LANDSCAPE ALCHEMY

THE WORK OF HARGREAVES ASSOCIATES

LANDSCAPE ALCHEMY

THE WORK OF HARGREAVES ASSOCIATES

**Contributions by George Hargreaves,
Julia Czerniak, Anita Berrizbeitia
and Liz Campbell Kelly**

ORO editions

CONTENTS

INTRODUCTION

GEORGE HARGREAVES

I am very pleased to introduce this monograph of the work of Hargreaves Associates. It contains a selection of projects representing the firm's work over the last two decades, including built and unbuilt work at varying scales and encompassing a range of landscape typologies. The book looks to the past, to the current moment, and to the future, tracing the trajectory of the firm from its early days through to recently completed major commissions and competition submittals. Organized into chapters around six themes, photographs and drawings of the projects are presented with accompanying text that gives context and describes the major design strategies for each. The monograph operates in the first pictorially, representing the works with images. For those who wish to dive deeper, this visual presentation is supported through the textual information and three essays that take a closer look at the firm's work and larger role. The first, by Anita Berrizbeitia, discusses key concepts that give insight into the work of the firm. She brackets her discussion of our evolving design philosophy with two essays – one is an early essay I authored in the first years of the firm and the second is my recent chapter in the book Large Parks, co-edited with Julia Czerniak. These two essays act as markers to give context to the consistent themes of the work of the firm and as their relationship to the recent history of landscape architecture practice. In the second essay, Czerniak uses our public projects as a fulcrum to discuss parks as active agents of transformation and revitalization

of the city. In this essay she posits the quality of design as a direct cause of the economic and social success of the park. The last essay is by Liz Campbell Kelly, a relative newcomer to landscape criticism, whose concluding remarks look to the evolution of the firm's design philosophy over time into her description as a "maximal practice." I would like to thank all three writers for their time and continuing insight.

Design Strategies

This firm has never seen a greenfield or "natural" site for its work. Our sites are brownfields, often flat, devoid of any significant vegetation or other natural features, yet close to city centers. These late 20th and early 21st century sites differ greatly from the majority of the sites for the great parks realized from the 17th to early 20th centuries. The earlier park sites had much more obvious character, a latent structure of topography, geology, ecology, or the traces of past uses accrued over time. The ancient forests of Bois de Bologne, the serpentine at Hyde Park, and Central and Prospect Park in New York, with glacial terrain and remnant countryside, all provided underlying conditions, what I like to call "good bones," for the mature parks they would become. For Hargreaves Associates, the history of our design strategies can be seen as a continuing search for the way to conceptually enter the site and create bones where there are none.

Initially we looked to environmental phenomena as a way to breathe life into dead and discarded sites. On smaller and mid-size projects, site histories formed narratives that created the projects' foundations. As the intricacy, scale and consequences of projects increased, we began to use a design strategy of measurement, though many people call this "program." Measurement works over distance and over time. When faced with a three-mile river that required flood control, as in Guadalupe River Park, measuring the volume and speed of flows of water led to a comprehensive and holistic system that acts across the board with a catalog of design solutions for specific circumstances employed wherever necessary. Time is another aspect of measurement. The events of our culture are often gauged through their own version of metes and bounds: recreation, festivals, concerts, performances, and gardens, to name a few, have a cyclical character that marks our lives. In the firm's work we use these events as active agents of design, permeating our parks with these displays of culture. Further, we juxtapose the adjacencies of a highly programmed use with natural systems – sculpture garden next to concert lawn next to wetlands. This strategy heightens the experience of the park and gives visibility to the connections between natural systems and culture. Within smaller urban parks, given the task of revitalizing the urban district and creating dynamic life, a richly laid tapestry of these measurements creates a robust urban form without an overwhelming multiplicity of landscape typologies.

Sustainability is basic to our projects and is permeated throughout them, but does not form the underlying driving design strategy. For the firm, sustainability functions at the same level as grading, planting, and drainage. The larger strategies create structure and the concept of the project, and the materiality of the site, including sustainability, supports the larger concepts and structure. None of these strategies – phenomena and process, site histories, adjacencies and overlays – operate singularly. Most often, these strategies interact on the same site as we strive to put bones in our projects that will give them life for decades or even centuries to come.

Identity

I came to an appreciation of the history of landscape architecture later than I should have. After practicing for several years I became intrigued with the longevity of public spaces. What made them a significant part of the community? What made them a valuable resource that led the public or a private entity to fund for their care and upkeep? If I could sum it up in one word I would choose identity, or if given two words, singular identity. The great public spaces of history were engendered by an active relationship with the mind of a city or region,

creating a unique place particular to local conditions of all kinds. The public landscape (often the park) occupies a distinct place in the urban environment, belonging to its community and no other. I believe this singularity comes about through several means. Legibility is a key ingredient. The visitor to the park must be able to decipher how the landscape reads within its context, and how it is special and different from other landscapes. For the firm this has always led us to a site specific or site generated response to a site, which acts to ground the site in the local. Durability is another main ingredient. The public landscape must be able to withstand use and the manner in which this is achieved becomes a key ingredient to the design process. Hargreaves Associates has found it critical to synchronize the design, management, and maintenance of any public space in order to achieve lasting durability. As the practice has evolved, strategies for durability become embedded into our conceptual thinking of the project. This can be manifested in flexible phasing, which ensures that the management of the place must be responsive to changing needs, as well as strategies for economic sustainability, which also require active management on a site that changes over time. Another ingredient is longevity. Can the park or other landscape type function

from one generation to the next, and can it perform in one moment at different levels for diverse age groups and ethnic backgrounds? This concept argues for creating varying, diverse landscape spaces, types, and experiences within one public space. The park is special to the individual in their experience of the moment and at the same time it is part of a collective consciousness. To consider the landscape a success, everyone must know it, yet it will be used for many purposes at any time. As we look forward as a firm we hope to create public spaces with singular identity, to make extraordinarily significant contributions to our culture, the holistic environment we live in, and the day-to-day life of each person.

The projects depicted and describe here are a team effort. Without the many employees, present and past, our work would not be of the quality I believe it to have achieved, or as wide-ranging and encompassing in terms of project types and scales. In particular, on behalf of myself and Senior Principal Mary Margaret Jones, we would like to thank the principals of the firm who lead each project. Without their hard work and unflagging efforts this monograph would not be possible. Finally, we would like to thank our clients who dreamed with us.

EARLY DAYS

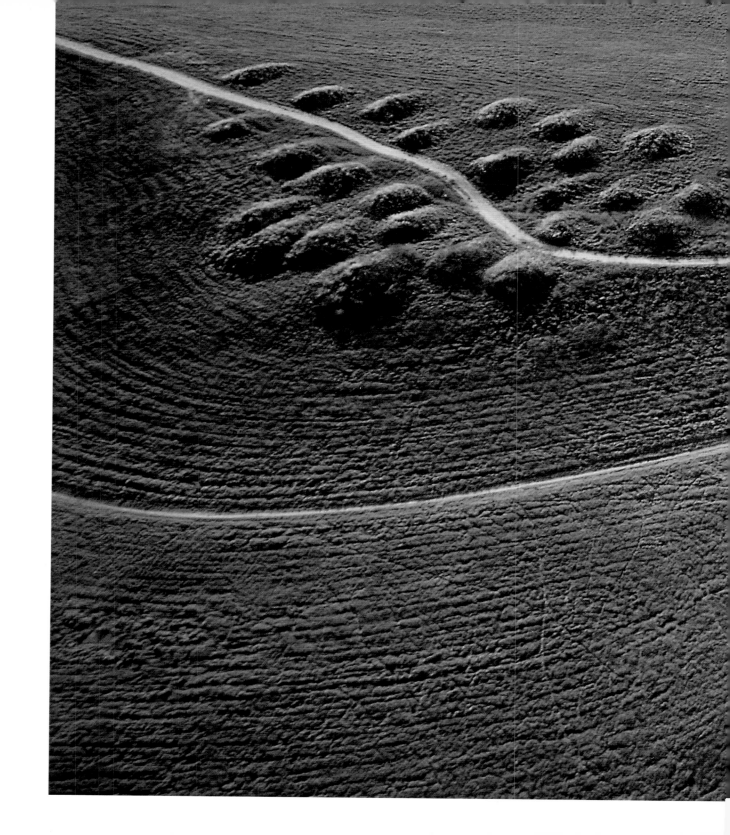

The early works of Hargreaves Associates are benchmark projects, creating identity for a young firm and in powerful design moves, generating the fundamental strategies that would guide future work. These early projects were testing grounds for ideas that chiefly looked for new ways to imagine landscape architecture beyond the formal compositions of modernism, the prevailing practice at the time. The firm looked to the site – its histories, ecological processes and visceral phenomena – to shape the narrative and form of the site design. This narrative based strategy and its elemental material palette created new vocabularies for public space, and reimagined the potential of the constructed landscape.

When Hargreaves Associates launched their practice in 1983, conversations in contemporary art and architecture created a widening discourse moving away from modernism. In architecture, postmodernism struggled to find a design language that referenced historical specificity, and loosened the formal strategies of international style modernism. Hargreaves Associates also looked to art, whose dialog around site specificity and earthworks, provided touchstone ideas for new design

01

constructions of site. The earthworks artists Robert Smithson, Michael Heizer, and Walter De Maria inspired the firm to shift their understanding of the materials of landscape towards the elemental – earth, sky, water and environmental phenomena[1]. The work of Robert Irwin, particularly his writing on site specificity in sculpture,

prompted Hargreaves Associates to look at strategies that are generated from the conditions of the site itself, rather than superimposing an independent idea or form onto a landscape. [2] This site-generated approach would become a touchstone idea for the firm and manifested itself in many of their early projects.

01: Plantings and path find new form at Villa Zapu. 02: At Plaza de César Chávez an interactive fountain surges and then disappears into fog. 03: The fountain is positioned at the crossroads of historic alignments.

02

03

01

The firm began working on **Plaza de César Chávez** (originally named Plaza Park) in 1986 in San José, California. The historic plaza was established by the Spanish as the town square in 1797 when, after twenty years on the banks of the Guadalupe River, artesian wells were found at this new location. The plaza played an important role in the history of California as the seat for the state government from 1849 to 1851. Currently the plaza is the home of several of San José's civic and cultural institutions including the City Government, San José Museum of Art, and the Tech Museum of Innovation. With the growth of the computing industries and the development of San José as the capitol of Silicon Valley in the 1980s, the redevelopment of Plaza de César Chávez was initiated as the centerpiece of a downtown rejuvenation strategy.

This early project demonstrated a narrative-driven design strategy, rejecting a resolved plan-oriented composition. Readings of history, and specifically the historic role of water on the site, provide the structural organization of the park – its overall layout, circulation, features and materiality. The design references the history of water in the semi-arid area – the Spanish settlement of the city and region, and the development and disappearance of agriculture in the region. The artesian wells on site made agriculture possible through irrigation. The irrigation of the Santa Clara Valley changed the figure of the land permanently, creating a cultivated landscape of fruit and almond trees. Hargreaves Associates present these histories overlaid with the new industry of technologies of Silicon Valley.

At the crossroads of the park an interactive fountain brings water to the surface, a metaphor for water on the site. Like the historic artesian wells, the fountains surge and then disappear into fog. The fog references the daily climate patterns of the Bay Area, and also cools the sunny site. A grid of lights overlaid on the fountain illuminates the feature at night and symbolizes the role of technology in Silicon Valley. This area is a nexus for the site, a natural gathering place for local families to enjoy an urban beach in the middle of the city.

The major circulation axis of the site, a central promenade marks the historic Monterey Highway, which connected Monterrey and San Francisco. Along this circulation path a grove of Jacaranda trees references the fruiting trees that once contoured the entire Santa

01, 02: Along the central promenade at Plaza de César Chávez a grove of jacaranda trees references the fruiting trees that once contoured the entire Santa Clara Valley.
03: The illuminated fountain gives contemporary form to both the historic artesian wells and the high tech future of Silicon Valley.
04: A collection of mature native trees root the park in the local.

02

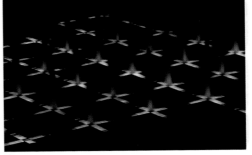

03

04

01

02

03

Clara Valley. Hargreaves Associates preserved a collection of mature California trees at the northern edge of the site – Redwoods, California Sycamores and Palm trees. These trees link the plaza to its past uses and existing structure, further constructing the palimpsest of the site.

While the site references the past, it also looks to the future. Hargreaves Associates created design elements within that park that give it structure and provide for the recreational needs of the urban community. At either end of the plaza a large stage and a smaller plinth receive gatherings – planned and impromptu. The large stage is programmed throughout the summer with musical and theatrical events.

The narrative strands of the park are spatially juxtaposed to deepen the sense of history and connection. The historical content of the site constructs a palimpsest, transformed into material through fountains, lights, promenades, and groves of Jacaranda trees. By juxtaposing the past and future through built material, the park is able to speak to the shifting socio-economic conditions of San José and look to the future possibilities of the city. At Plaza de César Chávez, site history becomes site form. In a break from the formalist strategies of the time, the structure of the site is both physical and narrative, rather than tied to a strict plan composition.

The firm pursued further breaks from modernist design strategies at **Candlestick Point Recreation Area,** on a windy site on the San Francisco Bay. Hargreaves Associates was part of a collaborative team with architect Mark Mack and artist Doug Hollis to create a design for the twenty-acre bayside site. Rich with environmental phenomena and low on budget, the project called for an experimental approach. Focusing on the intense winds of the site, the design team investigated ways that large scale sculptural interventions in the landscape could harness the environmental phenomena and guide the visitor's experience of the site. The large-scale earthworks are open to the natural processes of the extreme environmental conditions and the site is designed to change over time.

The designers were influenced by the works of the earthworks artists of the 1960s and 70s, including Smithson, Heizer, and de Maria. Through the earthworks artists, Hargreaves Associates saw how landscape architecture could create a new kind of powerful, moving landscape experience by using the materials of the earth itself. The earthworks at Candlestick Point emerge as *figured ground,* creating a sculptural encounter in the landscape and displaying a hybrid condition between art and landscape.[3] At the same time, the earthworks are designed towards the specific ends of a public space, inherently oriented to function. This expanded

field of landscape architecture, in this case achieved by the appropriation of the language and form of art, is an example of how Hargreaves Associates positioned themselves away from formalism, blurring the boundaries of the medium, creating powerful landscape experience that is still legible as park.

Like Plaza Park, the site design moved away from a plan based composition. At Candlestick Point, the designers focused on the individual phenomenological experience of the site and created a design with a site-generated

04

05

01-03: Large scale sculptural interventions in the landscape harness environmental phenomena at Candlestick Park. 04: Aerial view 05: Landform meets Bay.

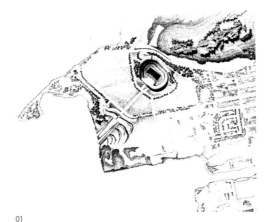

01

approach. Over a series of visits, the design team developed a way to view and experience the site through the visceral action of the wind. Arriving on the site, the design team would park at the edge and walk to the water with a strong wind at their backs. After many visits this experience developed into an idea to intensify the effect of this phenomenological sequence of the wind carrying the visitor to the water. The designers created a wind gate at the entry point. Walking through the wind gate leads to a large plane that gradually slopes to the water and tapers, accentuating the perspectival perception of the space.

Wind dunes flank the inclined plane, providing shelter from the wind after having the experience of being immersed in it. The minimal intervention in the landscape creates a transformative landscape experience.

The design team sought to open the park to the environmental processes of the Bay, setting in motion an overall form of the park that would change over time. Carved inlets allowed water to come into the site through the action of the tides. The tidal action continually shapes the form of the site. The design uses native plant communities to occupy the space, left to thrive where the conditions allow it. At Candlestick Point, the designed interactions with environmental processes create a large-scale phenomenological landscape that emphasizes the individual experience in a composed yet open-ended landscape.

The break from modernist formalism came to full fruition with **Byxbee Park.** Like Candlestick Point, Hargreaves Associates used a site-generated approach, organizing the design around specific moments of exploration on the site. Hargreaves Associates collaborated with two artists – Peter Richards and Michael

Oppenheimer – in the design of the site. In a similar process to the exploratory phase of Candlestick Point, the designers visited the site to sense its opportunities, developing the inherent qualities of the site into a sequence of design interventions.

Byxbee Park was a capped landfill, limiting the possibility of shaping the land significantly. Within the overall topography the design team created small earthwork interventions – the hillocks, the field of poles, concrete chevron jersey barriers, and graded concrete terraces. The series of earthwork constructions guide movement across the site, a contemporary formulation of the picturesque – the landscape understood through movement.

While the site interventions suggest movement, they also speak to the site itself. The grid of telephone poles mark shifting elevations against the ground, and originate as a reference to the infrastructural landscape of power lines in the area. The designers incorporated the idea that as the landfill elements beneath the poles broke down, the ground would shift and the poles would reflect the changing conditions under ground. While the settling that was predicted by the

01: Plan of Candlestick Park. 02, 03: The park invites the tidal cycles of the San Francisco Bay, interacting with open-ended natural processes.

02

03

01

engineers on the project has not occurred, the poles still act as a device for understanding landform, creating a reference of the constantly shifting landscape.

The landscape interventions at Byxbee Park provide context for the site. The chevrons are composed of jersey barriers and mark the flight path to the Palo Alto airport, creating a landscape that responds to the sky. As the planes fly overhead, one begins to imagine what the site would look like from the aerial perspective. The site suggests a playful understanding of site and landscape architecture. With an open program, Byxbee Park is a destination for itself, a place to experience artful manipulations of the material of earth, sky and the perception of landscape.

Guadalupe River Park, in downtown San José, integrates a linear riverfront park through downtown with a comprehensive flood control infrastructure project. The flow of the Guadalupe River provides an underlying datum for the park, with the design rigorously engaging natural systems and ecological processes to react to the specific flow conditions across the entire riverbed. This site-generated design acts as green infrastructure, providing flood protection to the City while simultaneously creating a linear recreation corridor.

01: The chevron jersey barriers at Byxbee Park.
02: Aerial view

02

As a consequence of Silicon Valley development, San José faced increased flooding of downtown streets from storm events. In order to eliminate downtown flash flooding, the Army Corps of Engineers proposed seventeen-foot concrete floodwalls to move the water quickly through downtown. If this had been pursued, the resulting fast moving water would not allow stormwater to infiltrate on site, exacerbating larger stormwater management issues created by the new growth of the city, and would also destroy wildlife habitat through the downtown river corridor. Fortunately, the city of San José resisted cutting itself off from the historic river, and Hargreaves Associates was hired to create a park along three miles of river and to work with the Army Corps to solve the flood control problems without relying solely on concrete floodwalls.

01-06: Byxbee Park is organized according to specific moments of site exploration. 07: Plan.

07

01

02

03

04

Hargreaves Associates devised a design strategy that proposed a limited number of design solutions that would respond to specific local conditions of the river and its adjacent uses. At three linear miles, the sheer size of the park resisted a varied, detailed design of each precise moment of the park. Also, the flood control measures required advanced fluid dynamics and flood modeling that would treat the site as a whole. Rather than design specific moments of the project, Hargreaves Associates designed a strategy that layers the technical needs of the river stormwater functions with

a circulation system, materiality system and riparian planting system. This strategy treats the Guadalupe River as an underlay, with the designed overlay elements responding systematically to local conditions.

Hargreaves Associates worked closely with the Army Corps of Engineers to build an 80' long scale fluid dynamic model to test design strategies. On the whole, Hargreaves Associates had two conflicting goals – to keep the river's edge as natural as possible, infiltrating and recharging floodwater, and to channelize the river, moving the water

01-02: The grid of telephone poles at Byxbee Field mark shifting elevations against the ground. 03-04: The series of earthwork constructions guide movement across the site.

01

through downtown areas quickly to prevent flooding in the streets. To accommodate these two opposing goals, Hargreaves Associates designed combinations of smooth and rough areas, manipulating the speed of the water as it passed through key areas.

Water enters the designed park upstream approaching downtown. Much of the flowing water is diverted into a culvert and reintroduced upstream of Confluence Point where a wider dimension of the river could be created to accommodate the added flow. Through the urban downtown, a series of interventions structure the banks of the river and control the flow of the water. A gradient of textured surfaces – from gabions, step gabions, smoother stone terracing, and in one area a concrete wall – is deployed across the site to control the flow of water. The depth

and width of the river cavity also changes according to the desired flow of water and bordering land ownership. Where water needs to move quickly or be controlled, the riverbed becomes deeper and narrower. These techniques are also implemented around any crucial infrastructure, including the bridges that pass over the river about every two to three city blocks. After the water passes these key areas, the width of the river increases with a rougher planted surface and greater area for infiltration. The result across the whole of the site is an undulating river bank condition, allowing the river to function as a whole while reacting to immediate conditions. The portion of the river through the dense downtown had a smaller available width because of existing adjoining uses, which required a narrower, deeper channel with "hard" engineered surfaces. Downstream,

02

03

01: Aerial view of Guadalupe River Park. 02: The park acts as green infrastructure, providing flood protection and a recreation corridor. 03: Guadalupe Confluence Point.

01

02

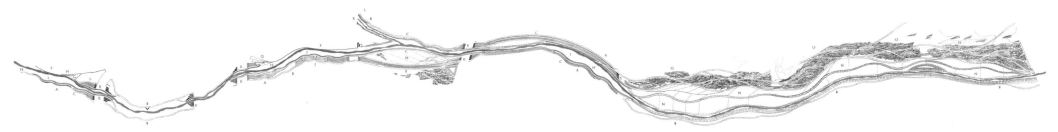

the river unfurls itself at the outskirts of the city, greatly enlarging the width of the river with "soft" engineered banks and a low-flow channel. In this area, Hargreaves Associates moved the river channel and widened the river corridor to accommodate the increased flow from downtown and planted the area with mitigation riverine vegetation, cultivating animal habitat. The adjacent parkland acts both as a recreation pathway and as a high-volume plane for the river. Hargreaves Associates designed a system of landforms and pathways that, when inundated, disperse the flow of water. The braided landform shapes mimic the stream morphology of the area and allude to the natural river condition. The park in this area is an open trail, used by walkers and bikers commuting to downtown.

Layered over the structure of the flood control measures is an ecological system of native, riparian plant species. The combination of conservation of the natural river edge,

01: Downstream the adjacent parklands act as a recreation pathway and a high-volume plane for the river. 02-03: Through the urban downtown, a series of interventions structure the banks of the river and control the flow of the water. 04: Plan.

03

04

01

02

03

and the construction of "soft" engineered edges work together to restore bird habitat to the corridor and to create a shaded riverine environment for fish spawning. The riparian plant species also are able to withstand periodic inundation associated with storm events. The circulation system of splitting paths gives pedestrians access to the site and negotiates the terraced river banks; when the river is high, the park is accessible on the upper paths. All site furnishings are flood resistant – lighting, benches, trash receptacles and handrails. These overlapping systems form a designed ecology of the river, which allows for the coexisting agendas of recreation, flood control, and plant community. These constructed systems transition into the larger natural system of the Guadalupe River as a whole. Rather than create site-specific interventions at the Guadalupe River, Hargreaves Associates designed a system that when deployed, creates a park, integrating natural systems with recreation, open to the flows of the river.

In these early projects Hargreaves Associates tested new ideas that in turn formed a foundation for future work. The projects and their methodologies represented a break from the formalist design strategies of modernism that landscape architects were practicing since the Bauhaus era.[4] The work of Hargreaves Associates in the 1980s and early 1990s created a language for landscape architecture to shift away from worn formal strategies into a new framework for constructing landscape architecture. The firm moved away from resolved plan-oriented composition and the objectification of site analysis towards open-ended spatial strategies. These early projects turned their attentions to new constructions of site-specificity, through *ecological process, environmental phenomena* and *cultural/historical readings*. Where previously the field had struggled, this approach was able to incorporate ecological design with human use and recreation, creating a practice that was equally sensitive to the ecological, historical and cultural meanings of place. Hargreaves Associates' investigations into site-specificity generated new vocabularies of the material of landscape. History, culture, environmental phenomena and process, and earthwork emerged as new materials to create significant works of landscape architecture. The early work of Hargreaves Associates put forth ecologically integrated, rigorously designed built landscapes that carry deep emotional power, revealing the connections between nature and culture.

CULTURES AND WATER

LOUISVILLE WATERFRONT PARK
Louisville, Kentucky

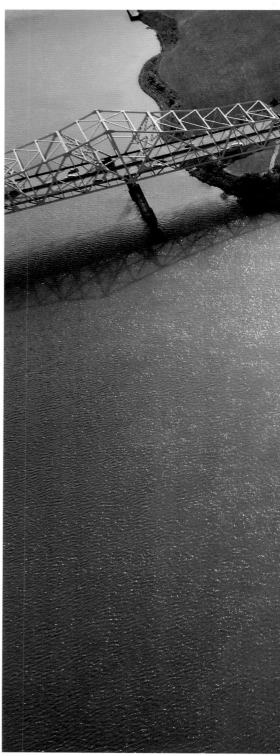

Hargreaves Associates' early projects established a working methodology that drew out the narratives of landscape through the skilled manipulation of earth, water and vegetation. As the practice developed, the firm designed a series of parks on brownfield waterfront sites. The waterfront park has developed out of the patterns of global post-industrial economies – the decline of industrial waterfronts, the exodus of urban populations to the suburbs, and the subsequent development renaissance as cities have worked to bring people from the suburbs back into the urban core. In the last two decades, landscape architects have increasingly worked at the urban edges of our cities, rejuvenating post-industrial sites for public use and catalyzing core urban renewal. Working at the waterfront, Hargreaves Associates has developed a core body of work, exploring cultural narratives of water while developing techniques for creating successful performative public space embedded in riverine systems and with lasting impact on its larger communities.

In these projects the firm continues to implement integrated natural systems based in phenomenological readings of the site. From earlier projects that primarily explore landscape process, these projects integrate comprehensive strategies that address access and program, bringing people to the site and providing a landscape structure to achieve a richer park experience for more established communities and user groups. As projects with specific development mandates from city agencies and public/private partnerships, the projects encompass sophisticated integrations of program able to reach highly diverse groups of constituents. A public process is vital to these projects in order to reach consensus within communities and key groups of stakeholders.

By the time Hargreaves Associates began work on the **Louisville Waterfront Park** on the Ohio River, they had already developed an approach that was particularly suited to the brownfield site. Their site-generated approach fosters projects that are transformative without erasure. At the post-industrial site, this approach privileges the deep connections between human culture and the development of economies of manufacturing. At the waterfront site, the approach seeks to enhance the bond between human culture and the natural processes that shaped the river over time, and the dynamic processes that continue to act on the landscape.

01: Model **02**: The park connects the street grid to the river's edge across a single slope, slipping under the elevated freeway.

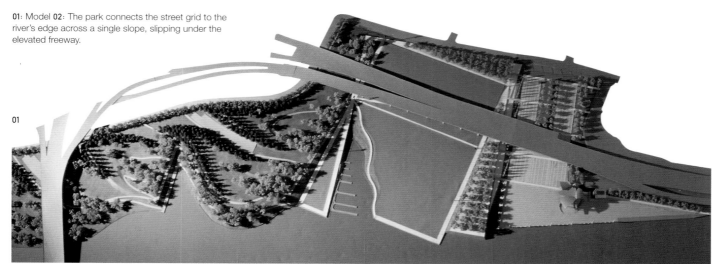

01

02

The city of Louisville was formed at the Falls of the Ohio, a series of limestone ledges dropping 26 feet in elevation. The Ohio was a major trade route and boats would have to portage around the falls until the Louisville Portland Canal was built in 1830. With the portage activity the city of Louisville formed around the Falls, developing as a major shipping port. Subsequent industrial activity centered along the river. The introduction of the railroad continued waterfront industrial use, as the tracks were built up along the river on 20 feet of fill to keep the rails out of the floodplain. In 1972, at the height of urban decline and the embrace of suburbia, the City of Louisville placed an elevated interstate (I-64) along the banks of the river, further cutting off pedestrian access to the river. With the decline of industry the waterfront also declined. Gradually, as "white flight" reversed itself populations started returning to the city from the suburbs. Now completely cut off from downtown, the focus of the Ohio River waterfront needed to be returned to Louisville. The Waterfront Development Corporation, a public/private partnership, envisioned the creation of the Louisville Waterfront Park to transform a postindustrial wasteland into an urban oriented park for the city, initiating a renaissance of public life in downtown Louisville.

Hargreaves Associates began working on the 120-acre project in 1990 with a master plan for the park. The firm worked closely with the public, holding over sixteen public meetings to develop the design of the park – understanding the needs of local residents, determining program, and providing a vision to the public of what the waterfront could become and how it could positively affect all of downtown Louisville.

The first objective at Louisville was to regain direct access to the river. The obstacles to direct access were River Road, a major road that cut the site off at grade level, the freeway that bisected the site overhead, and the twenty foot floodwall that formed the river's edge. Hargreaves Associates developed a comprehensive strategy to overcome these obstacles, first re-routing River Road through downtown to alleviate the barriers at grade, and then re-grading the site to allow direct visual and pedestrian access to the river from the entrance to the park. In a sweeping gesture, an inclined plane connects the street grid to the river's edge across a single slope.

01: The park transformed a postindustrial wasteland into an urban park for downtown Louisville.
02: Landforms create a sense of enclosure for the picnic area.

01

02

03

04

05

By making the river visible from the entrance of the park, the design removes the psychological barrier of the overhead freeway, and reconnects downtown to the riverfront, spatially and visually. The inclined plane, the Great Lawn, extends on hidden pylons out over the river creating a dramatic relationship with the Ohio River.

The grand planar geometries of the site negotiate the relationship to the Ohio River, inclining to meet the river, and tilting upwards to create tensions and distinctions between the programmed spaces. Sculptural landforms further shape the overall topography, designed to reflect the fluidity of the river and its dendritic patterns. Across the site carved inlets interact with the flow of the river, temporarily trapping and then releasing sediment and other debris illustrating the continuing natural processes of the river across a constructed edge.

The grading down of the Great Lawn to the river begins at the elevation six inches above the 100-year flood line, allowing the continuous plane to the river to act as a floodwall that protects downtown Louisville. The landscape is built to withstand temporary inundation, both the riparian planted edge and the Great Lawn, which is designed to drain quickly. Site furnishings are also designed to withstand periodic inundation. At the elevations up to the 10-year flood line, the park creates a riparian edge with native, flood-tolerant species, open to the waterborne seeds that inevitably sow in this zone.

01: The entry fountain brings a sculpted representation of the Ohio River into the park. 02: Pathways bring people to the river. 03: The industrial character of the site is transformed without erasure. 04: The Overlook rises from the park and affords dramatic views of the Ohio River. 05: The natural edge of the park is armored with hybrid engineering – geotextiles and rock filled gabions planted with riverine species.

01

01-02: The Festival Plaza at night.

02

Introducing open-ended natural processes to the park, this is a "landscape set in motion," increasing the richness and complexity of the designed landscape.[1] The lower banks, while appearing natural, are heavily reinforced with rock-filled gabion mattresses, geo-grid and geo-textile fabrics, inter-planted with native riparian species, and fortified with waterborne plants, creating a hybrid system integrating technologies with natural processes. Visitors explore the urban riparian edge on a pathway system that periodically links the upper and lower banks, crafting a complexity of vision through the continuously shifting relationships between river, city and the individual.

As the overarching planar geometries of the park create the basis of the revived relationship with the Ohio River, the development of program on site is instrumental in the crafting the narrative of site. In this project, Hargreaves Associates began to develop a strategy that accommodates multiple programs in one landscape typology, and furthered ideas of landscape juxtapositions that create tensions and meaning, earlier

implemented at Plaza Park. The Great Lawn is a programmable surface that allows for multiple activities from informal gatherings, sports to large events. The Festival Plaza supports smaller organized city-wide events, and the Overlook is a contemplative sculpture plaza with shaded seating at the water's edge, affording dramatic views to the Ohio River. These spaces are varied and open, accommodating multiple uses through a flexible structure. As the park moves away from downtown toward more residential neighborhoods, the program of the park becomes looser, emphasizing pathways for strolling, running and cycling, open meadows, a children's playground, and picnic areas. The success of the integrated program of the park proved a catalyst for the renaissance of urban life in Louisville. The park spurred development along the waterfront with several corporate headquarters, a baseball stadium, the Louisville Slugger Museum and a riverfront apartment tower. Access, program and process are the key elements that achieve success on the site, rejuvenating the waterfront district and celebrating the waterfront through a constructed edge open to ecological processes.

01

PARQUE DO TEJO E TRANÇÃO
Lisbon, Portugal

01-02: Landforms sculpt the site and create protected activity zones.
03: Dendritic landforms mimic the wind's movement across the site.
04: A marsh wetland returns habitat to the brownfield site.

02

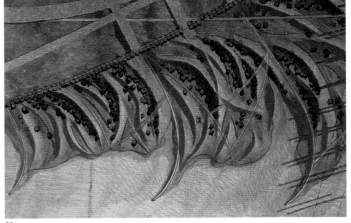

03

04

Working at another brownfield site, in 1994, Hargreaves Associates won an international competition to design **Parque do Tejo e Trancão**, a 160-acre environmental park developed in conjunction with the Expo '98, held in Lisbon, Portugal. Sited in an area of the city known as its garbage dump, with numerous waste treatment plants and landfills, the city used the Expo to transform the perception of this part of the city, developing the area with residential and recreational uses, including a major park at the waterfront on the site of a landfill. Parque do Tejo e Trancão was intended to act threefold – to create a new impression of the neighborhood, complement the pavilions for the Expo, and provide open space for the future life of the new residential units.

The site is located at the confluence of the River Tejo and the polluted River Trancão, on an industrial site that had been long abused. When the competition began the site consisted of a sixty-seven acre landfill, a sewage treatment plant, a solid waste treatment plant, and other industrial uses. The design approach addressed the environmental issues of the site and created a narrative based on a phenomenological reading. The design is rooted in an idea of castings, creating earthworks on site that respond to the landfill processes below ground and interpret the wind patterns above ground. The landforms were built with 500,000 cubic yards of sediment that were dredged from the harbor, creating a landscape designed to incorporate the changing conditions of the dynamic site. The design put forward a range of typologies of landforms. In the design the overall form of the site capped the landfill site below, and a series of earthen cones mask landfill monitoring wells and dendritic landforms imitate the actions of wind and water on site. Like Guadalupe

River Park, the form above ground reflects the conditions below grade in a site-generated design. The landforms act as markers on site, facilitating a range of active and passive recreation by creating areas of shelter from wind, and exposed areas to enjoy the outlaying views. Though the design for the park encompassed wide variations in topological forms, ultimately the full range of landforms was only partially executed. The design also re-created the native marsh ecology of the site, increasing habitat and treating water for the irrigation of on-site sports fields. The marsh is connected to the interior of the park by a promenade on land and over water. Parque do Tejo e Trancão transformed a maligned area of Lisbon for a major world event, and created a catalyst for ongoing residential development long after the Expo finished.

01

02

CRISSY FIELD
San Francisco, California

The integration of ecological habitat and recreation at a brownfield continued at **Crissy Field**. There, Hargreaves Associates found a deeply complex polluted site with passionate constituents who each had very different ideas for the future park. A National Park Service site on the San Francisco Bay, there were those that valued the site for its significant milestones in military aviation history, environmentalists that wanted to restore the fragile tidal marsh ecosystem, and active boardsailors and dog-walkers who wanted to maintain active recreation. All felt that their preferred use should be protected and expanded. The park design maintains a delicate balance of program, history, and ecology, juxtaposing these seemingly incompatible uses. The project successfully negotiates the environmental needs of an area with active recreation. The design for Crissy Field creates a finely balanced system of heightened proximities. These proximities act to enhance the understanding of the cultural and ecological significance of the site.

The Crissy Field site is rich in military and aviation history. The Spanish built the Presidio, a military installation, in 1776. The site was variously occupied by the Spanish, Mexican and American military until it was finally decommissioned in 1994 in a national round of base closures. The existing tidal marsh ecology of the site was completely filled in 1915 to build a racetrack for the Panama-Pacific International Exposition. After the Exposition the US Army converted this area into a grass airfield, the first on the West Coast, which became the site of many historic achievements in aviation. It was at Crissy Field that the first biplanes that flew to Hawaii took off, as well as speed record flights to New York. The military continued to use the airfield, entombing the original grass strip under asphalt and concrete. The military use of the site created significant pollution of the soil and groundwater, necessitating a cleanup as the first stage of the transition from military post to national park.

03

01: Crissy Field integrates ecological habitat with recreation.
02: The park is part of the Golden Gate National Recreation Area on the San Francisco Bay. 03: Aerial view of the park shows the historic airfield, tidal marsh and beach.

01

01-02: Landforms figure the site and provide protection from
strong winds.

02

01

01: A generous promenade unites the site, providing sweeping views to the San Francisco Bay and access to the spectrum of park uses. **02:** The historic airfield is an open space with flexible program. **03-04:** Local ecological communities are embedded into the fabric of the park.

02

03

04

In its latter stages as a military base, the military allowed for civilian use of the site to take advantage of the beach and stunning views to the Golden Gate Bridge. After the base was decommissioned, ownership of the site transferred to the Golden Gate National Recreation Area, administered by the National Park Service, and the informal use continued, primarily for boardsailing and windsurfing, where the typical wind pattern makes conditions ideal, and dog walking, where a fenced area allowed dogs to run off-leash. As the transition from informal uses to a formal park began, an extensive public process allowed the user groups to come together. The firm developed design solutions for the future park where all would compromise, and all would gain.

The Crissy Field design allocates distinct areas to each of the uses – a protected beach, an area demarcated for the tidal marsh restoration, the recreated airfield, and a picnicking area for passive recreation. A generous one-mile long promenade unites the site, providing sweeping views to the San Francisco Bay and access to the spectrum of park uses. Sectional grade changes and fencing hidden by planting allow the fragile tidal marsh to share its boundary with areas of active recreation – the beach for boardsailing and the historic airfield. By maintaining visual proximity but restricted physical access, Hargreaves Associates is able to layer and juxtapose the dynamic and sensitive ecology of the site with its historical meanings as well as active recreation use. This juxtaposition reveals the complexity of the site and its meaning, suggesting the interrelationships between ecology, culture and history.

01

02

03

An operations approach to the site contributed to a linear method of construction. First the promenade was built, so that parts of the park could be kept open throughout the construction process. Next, the twenty-acre tidal marsh area was excavated in order to create the wetland. The firm worked extensively with environmental engineers to first create a self-contained wetland before creating a channel that opens it to tidal exchange with the San Francisco Bay. The wetland was established with plants grown in nurseries at the Presidio. Once the wetland was mature, a channel at the eastern end was dug to open the marsh to San Francisco Bay.

The fill from the excavation of the tidal marsh was used to form the airfield as a subtle earthwork, thickened to emphasize its form and create a grade separation with the tidal marsh. The kidney bean shape of the airfield is derived from the wooden racetrack at the 1915 Exposition. The grade of the airfield rises from the airfield structures to the tidal marsh, creating an imperceptible rise on the airfield itself, but resulting in an eight-foot elevation change from the edge of the airstrip to the tidal marsh. This grade change at the edge separates the access between the airfield and the tidal marsh while maintaining their adjacencies.

The design demarcates a beach area for the boardsailors that enables easy launching of the boards into the bay and the best location for winds. Nearby parking facilitates the boardsailors, with an overflow area on reinforced turf. Responding to the dogwalkers, the Golden Gate National Recreation Area made special legal allowances to allow off-leash dog-walking at Crissy Field. The dogs are excluded from the tidal marsh through fencing that is concealed by the marsh vegetation.

04

05

01: The tidal marsh. 02: View to San Francisco. 03: Landforms shape the park experience. 04-05: Fencing protects native plant communities.

01

02

The first urban park in the National Park System, Crissy Field creates a unique experience of natural systems and history within the city. The design allows the disparate components of the site – ecology, history, culture – to co-exist as a cultural landscape. A strict re-creation of the past, either for the airfield or the tidal marsh would have been possible, but would have missed inherent opportunities to create interface between the uses of the site. Through materiality, grading and strategic juxtapositions the history of the site is read and the ecology is experienced. The earthwork form of the airfield marks it as a place of meaning with minimal explanatory signage. The tidal marsh has a functional value for wildlife, and also allows visitors to the park to experience an exceptional ecological habitat. Continuing the strategy of juxtaposition established at Plaza Park and Louisville, Hargreaves Associates pulls through the layers of palimpsest of the site. Transcending any prosaic idea of compromise, Crissy Field creates a reading of place that enhances cultural meaning and the vital connections between ecology, history, and every day life.

01: Windsurfers take advantage of ideal wind conditions.
02: The park juxtaposes a dynamic ecology with historical meanings and active recreation. 03: Moonrise over the airfield and tidal marsh. 04: The raised level of the airfield emphasizes its form. 05: At the West Bluff, landforms protect from winds and form zones designed for spontaneous use.

03

04

05

21st CENTURY WATERFRONT
Chattanooga, Tennessee

Extracting history from the ground, the **21ˢᵗ Century Waterfront** in Chattanooga, Tennessee, integrates waterfront development, ecology, history and everyday life. The parks at Chattanooga were preceded by a Hargreaves Associates master plan effort that sought a large scale rejuvenation of 129 acres of waterfront on the north and south banks of the Tennessee River. The masterplan effort identified a group of development sites for waterfront parks, and identified other residential and commercial parcels that could be developed in conjunction with the waterfront by private developers. In this way, private and public development worked hand in hand, enriching the economic viability of the city, linking the waterfront to Chattanooga's downtown core. Key infrastructural changes were also made to roadways, allowing the Riverfront Parkway to be moved and reducing the lanes from four to two. This move expanded the park width riverside, creating better access to the waterfront as well as additional development sites.

With the completion of the masterplan and initial infrastructural changes, the firm began work on the first major waterfront public park that was identified in the masterplan. Archaeological investigations of the site, mandated by the federal government, uncovered a fascinating history. The site was the location for Ross's Landing, the place of settlement by John Ross, the political leader of the Cherokee nation until 1838, when Native Americans were expelled westward under the Indian Removal Act of 1830. Ross's Landing became one of three trailheads for the Trail of Tears, the route west taken by Native Americans.

01: An amphitheater achieves access to the waterfront and doubles as a marina. **02:** The waterfront makes connections with Chattanooga's downtown core.

02

01

02

03

The design implements several strategies to incorporate these significant cultural elements, focusing overall concentration of the design to the Ross's Landing site. With a series of folded planes across the site, the design creates key moments of tension and compression that culminate at the Ross's Landing site. These tilted planes also work to bring the elevations of the park down to the river, providing circulation access and creating amphitheater landforms along the riverbanks. The open green space at Ross's Landing hosts festivals and other large events celebrating Chattanooga. A sculptural fountain using water from the Tennessee River memorializes Ross's Landing and celebrates Cherokee culture. Several city-wide events take place at Ross's Landing – the RiverBend Festival, which draws 60,000-70,000 people, and the second largest rowing regatta in the US, the Head of the Hooch.

Hargreaves Associates also worked closely with artists from the Cherokee Nation of Oklahoma to integrate their art with public space, commemorating the Trail of Tears. In an area called The Passage, the Gadugi artists created motifs that express and build on 1000 years of Cherokee art, celebrating the Cherokee culture that continues to flourish despite its hardships. Another public art project is situated along the Chattanooga Pier, which extends the streetscape 160' out over the River. Along the pier, light artist James Carpenter designed a series of seven 40' tall lighting elements that celebrate the access to the River.

01: Custom light elements celebrate access to the Tennessee River. 02: An allée frames a view to the fountains. 03: The sculptural fountain memorializes Ross's Landing. 04: The Passage brings water into the park and is a site for public art.

01

01: The large stepped amphitheater accommodates viewers for several river oriented city events. **02:** Tilted planes bring the city to the river.

CULTURES AND WATER: 21ST CENTURY WATERFRONT

01

02

03

01: The waterfront park re-engages the city with the river and its natural features. 02: The light pylons at night. 03: The fountain at Ross's Landing uses water from the Tennessee River.

The Tennessee River is a highly controlled river, under the auspices of the Tennessee Valley Authority and the Army Corps of Engineers. The river is manipulated for hydroelectric power, converting it during summer months into a series of flat lakes through a system of locks. The design implements a native plant strategy, riparian plantings and geo-textiles to reinforce the banks of the Tennessee. Structural moves improve animal habitat – insect, birds, amphibian, fish and mammal – at the river's edge. Moorings for boats create a pile-supported canopy over the river, which provides the ideal shaded habitat for fish in the river. The area is now a key spot both for riverfront boating as well as a popular fishing location.

Other key aspects of the project include the First Street Steps, which regain access to the Hunter Museum of Art and the Aquarium, reconnecting the museums to downtown. Steps and a funicular lead from the waterfront park to the site uphill. Working with private developers, the parcels along the steps were developed to introduce residential living to the waterfront district. The waterfront also connects across the river, to the north to Renaissance Park (see *Urban Parks*).

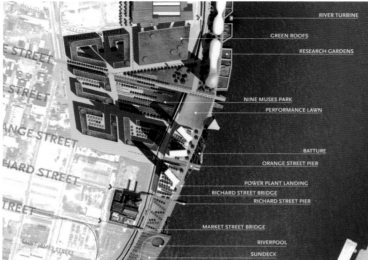

RIVER TURBINE

GREEN ROOFS

RESEARCH GARDENS

NINE MUSES PARK
PERFORMANCE LAWN

BATTURE
ORANGE STREET PIER

POWER PLANT LANDING
RICHARD STREET BRIDGE
RICHARD STREET PIER

MARKET STREET BRIDGE

RIVERPOOL

SUNDECK

01

RIVERSPHERE
9 MUSES SQ
CELESTE ST PARK
JULIA ST
BYWATER POINT
SPANISH PLAZA
POLAND FIELDS
JACKSON SQ
PIETY
ESPLANADE
NOCCA

02

03

04

NEW ORLEANS WATERFRONT: REINVENTING THE CRESCENT
New Orleans, Louisiana

01: Landscape at Market Street Promenade, Riversphere and Nine Muses Square. **02**: Six miles of public spaces along the Mississippi River integrates waterfront development with the core downtown. **03-04**: Reenvisioning Spanish Plaza.

At the 21st Century Waterfront in Chattanooga, a masterplan and park was able to significantly transform both the waterfront and an expanded area of development into the core downtown of Chattanooga. This integration of the development of the waterfront with the core downtown is also the goal of **New Orleans Waterfront: Reinventing The Crescent**, a masterplan for six miles of Mississippi River waterfront in New Orleans. Hargreaves Associates began working on the plan after Hurricane Katrina with a collaborative team of architects and planners. As New Orleans has suffered the slow loss of maritime activity and the crippling loss of civic vitality due to Hurricane Katrina, the project is an effort to inject renewed focus to the riverfront and spark investment in the city. The state and federal governments provided funding to make quality of life improvements to the riverfront along the southern edge of New Orleans, specifically

separated from funding of the recovery from Hurricane Katrina, which focuses on the northern region of the city, lower in elevation and adjacent to Lake Pontchartrain. The masterplan envisions an integrated residential and open space development of the industrial riverfront.

Paradoxically, the riverfront is the high ground of New Orleans, built up over the years to rise above the floodplain. Like other riverfront cities, there are significant barriers to access the river, though the obstacles here are particular to the unique delta conditions of the mouth of the Mississippi River. As a highly controlled river, state and federal regulations limit the developable land along the waterfront to twenty-two of the total 174 acres. Because of this restriction, the focus of the masterplan emphasizes continuous open space along the riverfront.

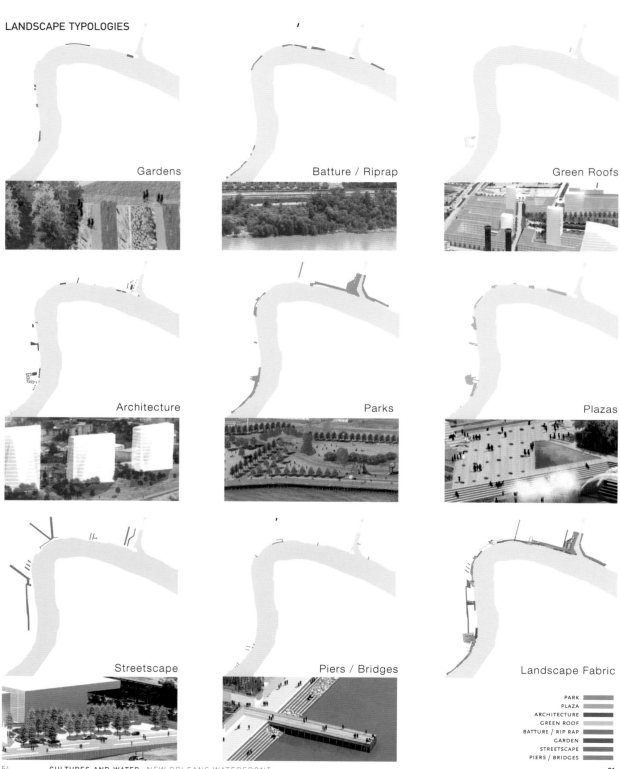

Gardens

Batture / Riprap

Green Roofs

Architecture

Parks

Plazas

Streetscape

Piers / Bridges

Landscape Fabric

| PARK |
| PLAZA |
| ARCHITECTURE |
| GREEN ROOF |
| BATTURE / RIP RAP |
| GARDEN |
| STREETSCAPE |
| PIERS / BRIDGES |

01

02

Currently, only ½ mile of six miles of waterfront is accessible to the public. Along with industrial wharves, most collapsed or not in use, and railroad lines that block access to the Mississippi, there are also significant earthen levees and floodwalls that obstruct views and access. The masterplan proposes a system of landscape and architectural structures as bridges over obstacles to give access to the river. *(p.55 fig 04)* These structures allow for a continuous accessible green public landscape along the full six miles of riverfront.

The landscape components of the development sites include connective streetscapes that lead to the riverfront, and riverfront parks that are composed of plazas, gardens, and areas of batture. Batture describes ecological zones formed in the alluvial lands between the Mississippi and the levee. New areas of batture will be formed with riprap, with sediment and vegetation accruing over time. These areas will act to restore habitat to the riparian edge. Piers and bridges will intermittently extend perpendicularly into the Mississippi, replacing the no longer active commercial wharves, previously used for the unloading and loading of ships. Looking to the culture of the city, Hargreaves Associates looked to the open structure of jazz in order to create a varied yet cohesive space across the six miles. Hargreaves Associates deployed a series of basic typologies of open space – Gardens, Batture/Riprap, Greenroof, Architecture, Parks, Plaza, Streetscape and Pier/Bridges – across the riverfront, creating a diverse fertile ground to restore active civic life to New Orleans.

01: The design looks to the open structure of jazz to deploy a series of open space typologies across the riverfront, creating a diverse fertile ground. **02**: Press Street Landing /Piety Park uses a building to bridge over rail lines and the floodwall to reach the river. **03**: Celeste Park features a wetland perched over the river. **04**: The design creates a system of landscape interventions to overcome a range of barriers to the Mississippi River.

03

Where site opportunities exist, the waterfront will support ferry terminals with tourist facilities, retail and commercial development and housing where the space allows it. The site is bookended with two major institutional projects. Tulane University and Xavier University will collaborate on Riversphere, a new environmental research and teaching center. The Nine Muses park area includes a large amphitheater and performance lawn that seats up to 5000 people. At the downriver end of the crescent, the New Orleans Center for Creative Arts (NOCCA) forms the other institutional bookend located at Press Street. A new facility for NOCCA has the opportunity to bridge over the railroad tracks, and create cohesive open space that ties into the programming of the cultural institution.

The Moonwalk site, near the French Quarter, contains the site of the founding of New Orleans at a natural levee, and provides a connection to the historic Jackson Square. Currently, Jackson Square is cut off from the Mississippi by a major roadway, parking lot and railroad. The masterplan creates, in one area, a pedestrian bridge over these obstacles, and in another area, a paving scheme that provides a wide walkway to cut through the roadway and railroad to the levee. Wide landscape staggered seatwalls reach down to the river, encouraging observation of the maritime activity. Shade structures along the levee provide shelter from the hot sun in summer. Overall, the connections to the river at the French Quarter are strengthened, enhancing the historic district.

Each aspect of the masterplan focuses on reintroducing access, recreating local ecologies, and forming a structure for rich social spaces. The diverse landscape typologies deployed along the riverfront avoid over-determined programming of the spaces. A layered composition of open spaces, Reinventing the Crescent creates new public space ready to be infused with the rich culture of New Orleans, and positioned to stabilize a city with an uncertain future.

FLOODWALL

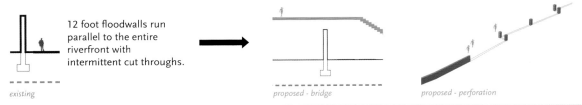

12 foot floodwalls run parallel to the entire riverfront with intermittent cut throughs.

RAILWAY/TROLLEY

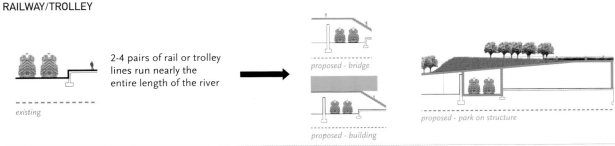

2-4 pairs of rail or trolley lines run nearly the entire length of the river

BOX LEVEE

The box levee is 2-4 feet higher in elevation than the cityside context.

WATER'S EDGE

Current conditions make access to the water's edge dangerous, illegal, or impossible.

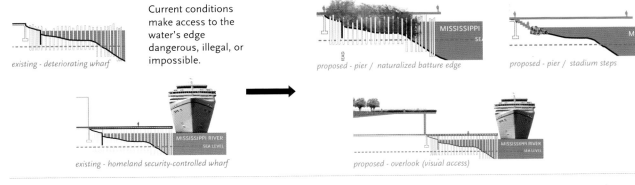

WAREHOUSE

Warehouses block visual and physical access to the river.

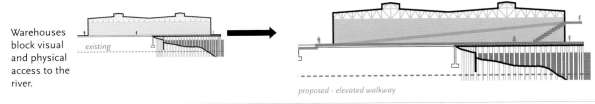

04

01

MISSION ROCK (SEA WALL LOT 337)
San Francisco, California

Waterfront parks can also be used as the focus of newly created urban neighborhoods. Hargreaves Associates won **Mission Rock (Seawall 337)**, a development and urban design competition in San Francisco, teamed with Perkins+Will and Beyer Blinder Belle for a consortium of developers including the San Francisco Giants. This project provides a development scheme for the last undeveloped parcel of Mission Bay. The site is built upon layers of fill from the rubble of early 20th century earthquakes in San Francisco and is adjacent to Pier 50 Mission Rock, the only outcropping of rock in the Mission Bay District. The design proposal takes this location into account by considering historic land use, and concepts of made land and expansion into the water for urban revitalization. The proposal plans a range of mixed-use housing and commercial buildings and a significant open space network.

The site is currently composed of sixteen acres of asphalt used as surface parking for the San Francisco Giants, whose stadium is located to the north of the site across Mission Creek. The overall strategy for the site creates a large aggregate five-acre open space at the northeast corner of the parcel, and integrates existing street grids into a new cohesive system that emphasizes view corridors. Placing the park at the northeast corner of the site creates a park that is a local amenity to the new mixed-use district and an attraction for greater San Francisco. The site maximizes the opportunities for the spectacular viewsheds into the San Francisco Bay, Giants AT&T Park and the central business district across Mission Creek to the north. This location allows for stunning views to fireworks, the sunrise over the East Bay, and the Oakland shipyards with large ships coming in and out of the bay. The western edge of the park is formed by the corridor to the Lefty O'Doul Bridge, which creates easy access to the north across Mission Creek.

The Bay Trail, a regional trail system at the San Francisco Bay, forms the eastern and northern edge of development and waterfront park. In the proposal, the Bay Trail takes the form of a signature promenade that provides an armature of program, viewshed, and engagement with the water at the linear edge. The promenade is a dynamic surface that engages the waterfront edge by stepping down to meet the water, creating amphitheater-like forms, stepping up to create picnicking areas, peeling off to form kayak launches, and splitting apart to allow for art installations that engage the water. The promenade, at up to eighty feet wide, allows for a highly programmed edge that engages directly with the waterfront conditions.

02

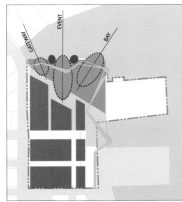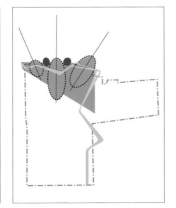

03

04

01: The waterfront park is the focus of the new planned urban neighborhood in San Francisco. **02**: The design integrates existing street grids into a new cohesive system that emphasizes view corridors. **03**: The site maximizes the opportunities for the spectacular viewsheds into the San Francisco Bay, Giants AT&T Park and the central business district across Mission Creek. **04**: The park is a local amenity to the new mixed-use district and an attraction for greater San Francisco.

01: The historic Pier 48 will be activated with new uses that can spill out onto the adjacent plaza. **02:** The Bay Trail is a signature promenade that provides an armature of program, viewshed, and engagement with the water. **03:** Plazas with dynamic fountains have a civic and urban quality. **04:** At the center of the urban design a neighborhood park features a flexible lawn bordered by retail and café spaces. **05:** The design proposes a dynamic and flexible event lawn that takes advantage of spectacular views.

03

04

05

Other urban design program elements for the site includes a mix of ground floor retail, office and residential uses. All parking, including that for the Giants ballpark, is in structures or below grade to emphasize a pedestrian oriented street district. There is a comprehensive sustainability plan that includes LEED Gold status for all of the buildings, greenroofs and on site stormwater treatment. A one-acre neighborhood park at the center of the development creates a small-scale neighborhood park for the development. At the eastern edge Pier 48 extends into the Bay and will provide a venue for events celebrating performance, art, recreation and food.

Hargreaves Associates has been instrumental in developing the scope and power of the post-industrial waterfront, rejuvenating brownfields sites for the public as cultural waterfront parks. At the waterfront, the firm has expanded early design approaches and interests into mature strategies for complex projects with major groups of stakeholders and highly coordinated economic development agendas. These parks have strong relationships with program, ecology and the urban infrastructure, acting in richly layered ways to enhance urban life. Through sophisticated, refined design, the resulting landscapes renew the connections between human culture and the natural processes of our waterfronts and have considerable impact on the economic viability of our cities. In an age of growing awareness of the necessity of environmental stewardship, they are areas vital to the reinvigoration of healthy interactions between humans and our ecologies. As the next era of life for our waterfronts, these projects explore the potential of the urban edge, inhabiting brownfields sites and seamlessly merging into the fabric of urban life.

KEY WORDS AND PHRASES

ANITA BERRIZBEITIA

Questions regarding the nature of landscape architecture, the quality and value of its ideas, and of the experiences it affords have been explored most prominently in the landscapes Hargreaves Associates have built, and that are documented in this volume. Yet the seeds of the ideas put forth in the projects appear in two essays that are relatively unknown, and that precede the built works. The first one, "Post Modernism Looks Beyond Itself" was published in 1983, the year the firm was founded.[1] The second one, "Large Parks: a Designer's Perspective," was written after twenty years of practice, in 2003.[2] A designer impatient with the written word who declared early in his career "[theory] doesn't count if you have not built it," George Hargreaves has written very little compared to some of his colleagues.[3] Nevertheless, these texts reveal the same spirit of critical reflection that has come to characterize their built work. In this essay I will situate the work of Hargreaves Associates through the lens of these two essays. Although they were not written with the intention of proposing an overarching design theory, they clearly define the issues that have guided and defined their practice thus far.

Early Years

In 1983, when George Hargreaves published "Post Modernism Looks beyond Itself," a paper that had been delivered at the American Society of Landscape Architects convention in Hawaii a few months earlier, criticism against the artistic orthodoxy of modernism was gaining full force among landscape architects. Martha Schwartz's Bagel Garden of 1979, her Necco Garden of 1980, Richard Haag's Gas Works Park of 1971-1988, and Hargreaves' (while still at SWA) Harlequin Plaza, to name a few, signaled the end of an era characterized by the uncritical acceptance of design methods that had been in place since the 1950s. The decade that followed the founding of the firm witnessed a reappearance of landscape architecture as a cultural discourse in its own right, with a broad range of design sensibilities that drew from larger cultural issues, producing a re-invigorated medium, and a great deal of self-consciousness about its own design languages and practices. A leading practice in this resurgence of landscape was Hargreaves Associates.

Like many young designers of their generation Hargreaves and his collaborators, Mary Margaret Jones, Glenn Allen, Gavin McMillan, and later an even younger group of principals in the firm, were deeply influenced by the earthwork artists, especially Robert Smithson, Richard Serra and Walter de Maria.[4] Specifically of Smithson's work, Hargreaves admired the way he "merge[d] his sculptures with site, to represent nature's ongoing and open-ended processes," and how they were formally incomplete, employing an "'open-ended' organization."[5]

However, for the theoretical and conceptual frameworks that form the core of his first essay, Hargreaves drew from the work of several art and architecture critics. Most notable, because of the influence they would exercise in the work of the first decade, are the writings of art historian Rosalind Krauss and artist/theorist Robert Irwin. Translating and making analogies between one medium (art) and another (landscape architecture) Hargreaves introduced a series of concepts that challenged accepted conventions in landscape architecture, and that became the foundations for their work.

The first challenge Hargreaves introduces in "Post Modernism Looks Beyond Itself" is against the spatiality of modern landscape architecture. The terms of this critique, learned from Krauss, were new to landscape architects, and were directed against landscapes that revolved "around an ***internal organization system***…in an idealized and invented space." With this phrase Hargreaves described what they did *not* want their work to become: inward-looking compositions disengaged from the external forces at work on a site. This was a provocative accusation, for modernism in landscape architecture was itself a reaction, exactly in the same terms, against the idealized invented space of Beaux Arts composition. Declaring that design begins with site and program, architecture and people, and not with composing patterns on the ground, Garrett Eckbo, James Rose and Dan Kiley argued during the late 1930s and early 1940s for a rational approach to landscape architecture that was hinged on the analysis of site, with forms that emerged from considerations of topography, orientation, context, and program, and not on abstract design. Still, for Hargreaves this was the case of one formal system replacing another, with both maintaining a philosophical and literal separateness from the real world outside. The content of these works fell ultimately on the forms themselves, and not on the larger subject of phenomena and its perception, of nature, or of history of the site, all of which would become central preoccupations of their work.

The alternative Hargreaves offered to the problems of idealized internal spaces was works that oriented to the outside, through **open-ended spatial configurations**. In Hargreaves Associates' work, open-endedness is a key term that holds multiple meanings. As language, it referred to the use of incomplete, yet bold and precise, geometric forms, such as segments of circles, asymmetrical landforms, or fields of arcs, that oscillated between their identity as (stable) object and open (occupiable) field. Organizationally, it referred to the use of repetition as a spatial strategy that avoided narratives of beginning, middle, and end, thus eschewing compositions that closed in on themselves. This additive strategy where there were no hierarchies, but simply a collection of things, one after the other, with no internal relationships between them, and no linear narratives, ultimately directed perception and interpretation away from those objects and into the landscape. Ultimately, it challenged the idea that the act of drawing a plan had to result in balanced, fully resolved compositions. In terms of design process, open-endedness meant that the types of things (ideas and forms) they would admit into their designs were not known a priori, but would be discovered in the process of historical and ecological research on the site. Open-ended formal configurations had direct analogies to ecological ideas, and the importance of this keyword is in fact as a bridge between art and ecology. Hargreaves Associates introduced the idea that formal open-endedness is a prerequisite for an appreciation of ecology. That open-ended formal configurations work to accept chance and change – ecology – in the landscape, by being receptive to time, to nature's processes, as well as to previous site narratives. Byxbee Park (1988) was the first project in which Hargreaves Associates was able to experiment with all of these ideas (fig. 1).

In plan it was unlike anything landscape architects had seen before. Neither geometric nor naturalistic, but with elements of both, it was strangely unfinished, made with a series of things, of unknown provenance, placed one after the other. That is, until one got there and walked through the site. Then the resonance between the site and its surrounding context became manifest, and revealed as the primary content of the work.

The idea that landscape architecture engages its site has been a fundamental value of the discipline, but by the 1970s, other than visually blending-in with the surrounding context, there had been no innovative ways to address the visual, cultural, and ecological features of the site. Hargreaves Associates questioned early on the conventional, and knee-jerk, response that to engage site meant to conform visually to it. Artist and theorist Robert Irwin, through his work and his writings, opened the question of the relationship between a work and its site to new interpretations that went beyond the visual. Especially useful was his distinction between site generated/specific, site conditioned, site adjusted, and site dominant works. This classification demonstrated different degrees of engagement between site and project that ranged from zero engagement to measurable gestures to the less tangible but more powerful psychological connections between the two. In adapting Irwin's theory to the complexities of landscape architecture, and to their emerging agenda of addressing complexity in the built environment, Hargreaves recognized that any one landscape is made of a combination of these different modes of engagement. Their ability to sort out, to combine, and to move from one to the other within one project made their work refreshingly articulate and varied while being fundamentally **site generated**. Guadalupe River Park (1988-1996) is a project that originates from the conditions that occur when two environments collide, an urban district and a river with severe flood cycles. Unlike conventional approaches in which a designer seeks a unified image for a river corridor, Hargreaves Associates accepted the changing character of the river along its three mile run. The result is a complex linear landscape that mediates between stable city and dynamic river, between intimate, lush, parkland and tough, monumental, urban spaces, and between experience and the pragmatics of flood control (fig. 2).

Fig. 1

Fig. 2

Fig 3

A fundamental ambition of the work of Hargreaves Associates is **presence**. Presence arises out of the seeming contradiction between a landscape's formal autonomy from its surrounding context – its refusal to blend in – and yet its complete integration with it, through the articulation of other forms of meaning. The key to this condition of autonomy from, and connection to, the surrounding landscape is their use of landforms as a primary structuring element of their designs. These landforms work to address multiple levels of meaning and experience. In terms of their size, scale, and physiognomy the landforms are clearly not mimetic. They do not resemble those that are the result of natural processes, like glaciation, erosion by wind or water, or fluvial depositions. Rather, they are the result of combining geometries of many types, using primarily clay models. Sometimes the landforms are performative, they need to guide flood waters, as in the Guadalupe River Park, and hydrologic engineering enters into the criteria of form making. Sometimes they pick up patterns outside the site, and stand as a reference for the site's context, as in Byxbee Park. Sometimes they address circulation flows, as at the heart of the Cincinnati campus. In all cases, they are the major structuring element, and constitute the primary image of the work. Further, the landforms are both vehicles for the landscape's autonomy – they resolutely declare their own artificiality – and for perception of time, place, ecology, phenomena. Beyond presence the work achieves a synthesis of what had been competing values between the artistic and the ecological.

The corollary of open-endedness is the externalization of **meaning**. Hargreaves proposes that the meaning of the work is not to be found within it, but relocated to the outside, to those things and attributes of the surrounding world that explain the work and give it its logic and poetics. "Natural elements abstracted or intensified, rather than imitated, can wholly reverse a works orientation from an internal idealization of nature to an external attempt at the reunion of human spirit and nature."[6] Herein lies the key to Hargreaves work, his forms, although to the untrained eye natural-looking, are not meant to signify nature. Rather, they are vehicles for the perception of phenomena such as light, wind, sound, moisture, seasonality, the life-cycles of plants, and the passage of time. Hargreaves Associates are less interested in the beautification of the site, and more interested in increasing the visitor's perception of the all encompassing power of nature around.

Recent Work

Twenty years after the publication of "Post Modernism Looks Beyond Itself," the issues facing landscape architects had shifted from a focus on language and expression, addressed primarily on small to medium sized sites, to questions of the transformation of large, usually post-industrial, sites into public landscapes. In "Large Parks: a Designer's Perspective" we see formal considerations momentarily suspended in order to examine the challenges posed by a specific landscape typology, public parks of at least 500 acres in size. Designing large landscapes challenged traditional values of landscape architecture that assumed that sites had to be completely re-made, and that the total transformation came from the directives of a master plan that contained in it all decisions, over the long duration, to be made on the site. This issue had been brought to the forefront of disciplinary discourse through a series of international competitions that were held in the United States, Canada, and Europe, starting in the early 1980s, on large sites that faced unpredictable futures and funding. These competitions rejected conventional master planning techniques based on formal structuring devices in favor of frameworks that allowed for flexibility, multiplicity, and program to emerge over time.

As he had done in "Post-modernism Looks Beyond Itself" Hargreaves began by examining a wide spectrum of precedents. Some were of sites that had persisted over the span of many centuries – such as the Bois de Boulogne in Paris and the Hyde Park system in London – maintaining their general ecological structure fairly intact. A second type of precedent entailed the complete transformation of the ecology of the site, from coastal sand dunes to pastoral park. A third type of precedent were sites transformed from one program to another, such as post-agricultural lands to parks (as in the Bos Park in Amsterdam and the Parc du Saussett in the outskirts of Paris), or from post-industrial lands to park (as in the case of the Landschaftspark Duisburg Nord). Here again, we see Hargreaves offering his critical reflections on a medium he believes to be at an important threshold in its development, a moment where the revision

HEREIN LIES THE KEY TO HARGREAVES WORK, HIS FORMS, ALTHOUGH TO THE UNTRAINED EYE NATURAL-LOOKING, ARE NOT MEANT TO SIGNIFY NATURE. RATHER, THEY ARE VEHICLES FOR THE PERCEPTION OF PHENOMENA SUCH AS LIGHT, WIND, SOUND, MOISTURE, SEASONALITY, THE LIFE-CYCLES OF PLANTS, AND THE PASSAGE OF TIME.

of its methods and ideas become critical to its development. As such, his readings of these sites are focused on the historical, social, and material processes that have led to their current state, probing on the causes and conditions that have propelled their evolution over time, as well as analyzing those elements that have persisted and that give them unique qualities. In this chapter Hargreaves re-examines some of the concepts he had been working with during the first two decades and, once again, introduces a set of ideas that forecast new directions of work.

The notion of landscape as **palimpsest**, as a series of layers that accumulate on a site over time, that are of different origins – geologic, social, productive – and that leave traces behind, has been a working assumption of the firm from its beginnings. However, in the earlier and smaller projects where the traces had been erased, Hargreaves Associates often reintroduced them as symbol, in order to reconstitute a site's complex history and unique identity. For example, in their San José Plaza Park the grid of Jacaranda trees and the central promenade bring back layers of the Spanish colonial occupation of that landscape, while the different effects of the fountain throughout the day are a reference to the city's varied histories, from geological times, to the present day. A similar approach, but with a much larger time scale as reference is their recent project for the Hudson Park and Boulevard (2008), titled Episodic Archaeology. In this linear park that extends between 33rd and 39th streets in New York City, Hargreaves Associates introduce a series of lost ecosystems and water that recall the pre-settlement landscape of Manhattan. The Hampstead Grasslands, the Pine Barrens, and the Tulip and Chestnut forest structure a narrative for the linear park that gives the site a new identity as it is transformed from a manufacturing and light industry district into a residential community. These are not literal reconstructions that attempt to reconstruct the past.

To the contrary, they remain unequivocally urban landscapes, informed as much by their ecological and cultural histories as they are by contemporary discourses on public space, urbanism, and their own aesthetic sensibilities (fig. 3).

Large landscapes, though, more often than not contain visible traces of previous occupations. They are powerful precedents through which Hargreaves demonstrates the legitimacy of their approach. In these cases, rather than introducing elements to construct a palimpsest, Hargreaves Associates works with the idea of heightening the expression of palimpsest already manifest in the site, a strategy that also builds on concepts of site-specificity. Of special interest to them is the history of topographical interventions on the site which leave lasting traces upon which new interpretations and uses continuously work to open the identity of a place. These traces, severed from their previous uses and associations, have been incorporated into their plans as found objects, with no authorial pedigree, a testament of the passage of time and to ongoing cultural processes on the landscape (figs. 4,5). Ultimately, this idea demonstrates a landscape's inherent **complexity**, a territory made by many parts of different material and historical origins that are in continuous, dynamic, and not entirely predictable interactions with each other. Hargreaves argues in "Large Parks" that the most compelling landscapes are those that overtly exhibit complexity, combining the wild, the cultivated, the recreational, the contemplative, the dynamic, the static. Design can foster and build complexity, paradoxically, once the designer relinquishes total control over the landscape in favor of a collaboration with it, one that is inclusive of both a complete open-endedness and precise, yet limited control, or that works with both processes and design operations.

Fig 4

Fig 5

Fig 6

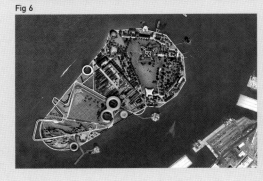

Landscape process, nature's progression through cycles of various scales – from seasonal ones, to plant succession, to adaptive change – reappears in "Large Parks" with expanded meanings. Whereas in the early years it was aligned with the firm's artistic agenda, as contemplative phenomena and content of the work, it is later presented as technique for constructing large ecosystems, and for managing change over the long term in the face of unpredictable economic changes and evolving cultural and social expectations for public space. From the poetics of process, then, we see a change to the pragmatic need for process. However, Hargreaves positions himself critically between a total commitment to process and an overly-specified plan. Rather, he advances the notion that to design large landscapes is to make decisions as to what part of a site remains open to process – underdesigned spaces that are open to unpredictable change – and which will be closed to them, as landscapes designed with full intentionality.

In opposition to process, **operations** are calculated procedures that stage those transformations necessary to establish specific relationships between existing and proposed ecological systems and programs in a site. Operations are performative, they accomplish intended effects, like introducing a new hydrological pattern on the site, they are connective, they work at different scales within a site, and over different time frames. Operations, as stand alone procedures or linked in a series, are key in their work because they allow Hargreaves Associates to intervene in both a systemic and a localized scale. That is, they allow them to insert a new structure in a site without having to remake the entire site. The combination of process and operations-driven design is a methodology that opens the door to complexity and long-term resilience in the landscape.

A **matrix** in landscape architecture refers to the dominant landscape type, such as a forest, a meadow, or a wetland, into which something else – program, topography, or other landscape – is inserted. What is important in this definition is that the matrix, while giving an identity and a structure to a landscape, also accepts difference within it in such a way that the identity of both (of the matrix and of the inserted thing) remains distinct.

This is crucial in landscape architecture because natural processes tend to blend everything together, and the articulation of the difference between the made and the existing quickly disappears. In "Large Parks" as well as in their recent work, Hargreaves introduces the idea of designing with multiple matrices within one site as a strategy for building complexity.

Conceptualizing a site as a series of different matrices that exist side by side and that are connected by a series of linked operations allows them to strategize their intervention in large landscapes in a manner that avoids the need to re-make and unify the site. In addition to being a strategy that enables a middle ground between the totally designed and the totally open matrices, for Hargreaves, are also potentially linked to site narratives, especially in those landscapes that are transformed from one land use to another. In those cases, introducing matrices that reconstitute different stages in that landscape's trajectory – primeval forest to agriculture to urban park – work in a similar way than the palimpsests, as a strategy that recovers the unique identity of that landscape (fig. 6).

Ecology, the study of the relationships between living organisms, is the fundamental building block of landscape architecture, and is cast as an inevitable and pragmatic, rather than political or philosophical, issue in the work of Hargreaves Associates. In their recent work its related concept, **sustainability**, has been at the center of their formal, programmatic, and technical explorations. Sustainability is generally defined as the use of natural resources such that they are allowed to renew themselves, without compromising their availability for future generations. All of Hargreaves Associates recent proposals include extensive provisions for those landscapes to produce their own energy supply, to cleanse their water, to store it for future uses, and to provide a recreational program that is adaptive and financially sound. Solar collectors, wind turbines, infiltration basins, native plantings, porous pavement, and the selective re-use of existing site structures, to name a few, have become standard elements of their proposals. These, however, are not merely accommodated for in the plans. They are made part of the experience of the place by being incorporated into design language, achieving a powerful synthesis of the techno-green-sublime that has come to define our times (fig.7). Hargreaves Associates also address sustainability by refraining from making decisions on all future uses of the site, leaving areas unspecified. For example, at Orange County Park, there was an ecological requirement to restore the meadows and an equally significant need to introduce recreational activities. Acknowledging the fragility of the oak savannah ecosystem, Hargreaves Associates avoided the conflict between preservation and social occupation by introducing a third option: a series of self-contained "pods" that will emerge as the community's recreational aspirations are identified. In this way, the savannah will developed undisturbed, while the needs of the community are met gradually as they arise (fig. 8).

Finally, **program**, the series of activities that are provided for in a park, has been a continuous subject of inquiry for the firm from the beginning. Although Hargreaves did not address the issue of program explicitly in "Post Modernism" he criticized modernism's reductive approach to program in a short commentary published in *Landscape Architecture* a few years later, in 1986.[7] During the early years Hargreaves Associates turned program emphatically away from the functional diagram toward the construction of meaning: landscape itself became the program. In the Louisville Waterfront Park, a 120-acre post-industrial site, Hargreaves Associates introduced the strategy of juxtaposing landscape typologies in order to facilitate program. The great lawn, festival plaza, marina, elevated play meadows, riparian edges, and the more intimate contemplative spaces are all sited abutting each other, rather than strung along a path in the traditional "necklace" plan. The same approach was used successfully at Crissy Field, Discovery Green, and, most recently, in the Governor's Island competition proposal. Here, Hargreaves Associates organizes the 172-acre island as a sequence of landscape types, pines and meadow grasses, beaches and dunes, orchards, athletic fields, park grounds, that from a varied matrix that responds to both the ecological structure of the island and its cultural program. A monumental promenade around the periphery of the island weaves in and out of the edge, alternating the visitor's views between inland landscape and open water expanse. The promenade itself acquires different character as it extends over the water, travels into the dunes, or becomes architecture. Boulevards that cut through the island are conceptualized as programmatically hybrid: they are simultaneously visual axes that connect the island with landmarks on the harbor, connective corridors between opposing ends of the island, urban terraces, and infrastructure (water + energy) corridors. The programmatic and functional multiplicity of each landscape type further augments the relationship between program, place, and experience. Hargreaves *composes* with program, rather than merely making room for it in the plan (fig. 9).

It is remarkable that both essays, in spite of being written two decades apart, end in the same way: as an open question and a challenge to themselves and their colleagues. In "Post Modernism" Hargreaves calls for, and forecasts, a field open to explorations of many kinds, full with potential for renewed meaning. In "Large Parks" Hargreaves anticipates the need for more creative uses of program, for a balance between process and form, between the uncritical preservation of sites, the reification of environmental guilt and social needs. Both texts were written at moments of significant transition for the firm and the field at large. They reflect a practice that has remained vigilant to the economic, ecologic, social, and aesthetic trends that shape the environment, addressing new imperatives while maintaining their commitment to the delivery of meaningful experiences. Their landscapes are both measures of changing sensibilities, and harbingers of things to come.

Fig 7

Fig 8

Fig 9a

Fig 9b

UNCOMMON PLACES

UNIVERSITY OF CINCINNATI: MASTERPLAN
Cincinnati, Ohio

01: The masterplan guided a transformation of the campus from a fragmented collection of academic buildings to a cohesive, connected urban campus. 02: Campus open space is connective and figural.

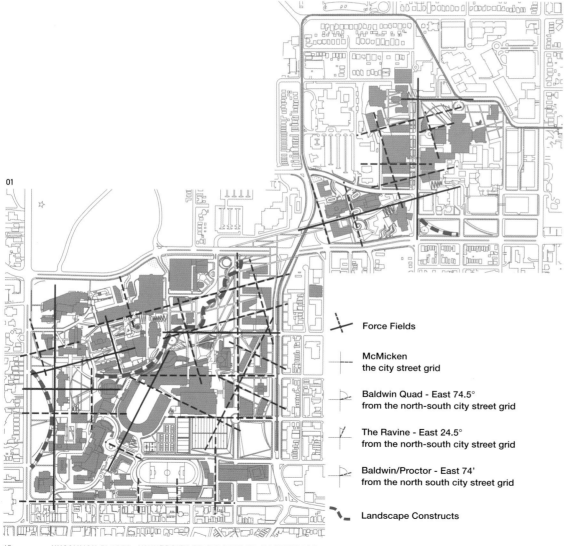

01

Force Fields

McMicken
the city street grid

Baldwin Quad - East 74.5°
from the north-south city street grid

The Ravine - East 24.5°
from the north-south city street grid

Baldwin/Proctor - East 74'
from the north south city street grid

Landscape Constructs

The idea of site is a central concept for landscape architects. From their very first projects, Hargreaves Associates established a working methodology that looks to site to find the essence of design – its motivation and manifestations. The early works of the firm were profound, in part because they moved beyond prevailing design practices that imposed autonomous form and composition. The firm's approach has consistently generated design from the phenomenological readings of place, as well as its embedded cultural histories. As the firm developed, increasingly sophisticated ideas of program were incorporated into the phenomenological and narrative designs. While each work of landscape architecture has unique site conditions, occasionally projects will have remarkably dramatic site conditions or exceptionally unusual program requirements that bring about extraordinary works of landscape architecture. *Uncommon Places* describe projects that fall into this category: a singular university campus, an Olympic park, a park for a presidential library, an art installation, and a precise and expansive environmental restoration park.

Hargreaves Associates participated in the continuing development of the **University of Cincinnati** campus for nearly two decades, beginning work on the first masterplan in 1989, overseeing a complete transformation of the campus from a fragmented collection of academic buildings to a cohesive, connected urban campus. The first masterplan, completed in 1991, develops a two-fold strategy, *infill* and *connection*, to create a cohesive campus. The second masterplan, completed in 1995, more fully developed implementation strategies. The third masterplan in 2000 focused on creating a twenty-four hour campus, transitioning from a commuter campus to a residential one.

01

02

03

UNIVERSITY OF CINCINNATI:
ARONOFF CENTER FOR DESIGN
Cincinnati, Ohio

Alongside the masterplan process, the University of Cincinnati made a significant commitment to architecture and design. In executing the masterplan, the University commissioned many prominent architects, including Peter Eisenman, Morphosis, Michael Graves, and Frank Gehry, to design signature academic buildings on the campus. In addition to developing the masterplan, Hargreaves Associates designed all of the significant open spaces on campus. Main Street, the signature and culminating project that specifically addressed the campus' desire for an activated, twenty-four hour campus, was completed in 2005 and its form guided the development of the Morphosis' Campus Recreation Center, the Tangeman University Center by Gwathmey Siegel and the Steger Student Life Center by Moore Ruble Yudell Architects & Planners.

While the university was established in 1819, there had not been an original campus plan that provided a long-term structure for growth. The historic campus had quadrangles framed by large buildings, where open spaces gave form to the buildings. However, after World War II, a population boom resulted in haphazard growth with buildings being erected

in whatever space possible, and surrounded by parking. The result was a fractured campus with buildings that did not have a cohesive relationship to each other, and had been sited without regard to the overall figure of the campus. Any open space was relegated to leftover spaces at the edges of the campus. This disorganization gave rise to the opportunity to create a new kind of contemporary campus, a distant cousin to the traditional quadrangle. The first masterplan proposes a strategy of *infill* to create a cohesive campus over time, emphasizing density over sprawl. Because the new infill buildings would be placed between existing buildings in already ad hoc site configuration, the new buildings would not necessarily have four sides. This results in a set of non-traditional building forms, amassed in relationship to each other and to site, creating a cohesive overall structure.

The other core principle of the masterplan is *connectivity*, both in circulation and design, as well as in ways that merge with the curriculum of the University – connecting students with faculty, connecting indoor and outdoor academic spaces. The overall circulation connections were challenging to make

01-04: The sculpted landforms work in concert with the Peter Eisenman building's interactions with site.

04

in a car-oriented culture with a hilly terrain. Rather than walk between classes, students would drive from parking lot to parking lot as they changed classes. Before a pedestrian circulation system would be used, Hargreaves Associates needed to create a parking strategy that would support a pedestrian-oriented open space strategy. The design eliminated the scattered surface parking lots across the campus and concentrated parking into four parking structures at the edges of the campus. This created open space at the interior of the campus, and encouraged pedestrian circulation over car culture.

Another important move created connection between the campus' two superblocks – the academic core (West Campus) and the Medical Campus to the northeast. Hargreaves Associates worked with the City and the University to simplify the intersection that connects the two superblocks. The new intersection released a triangle of land for open space that, with University Commons, now acts as a gateway between the campuses. The masterplan dictates a continuous tissue of open space that originates with McMicken Common, finds urban form at Main Street, transitions at Sigma Sigma Commons and leads to Campus Green, which

in turn leads directly to University Commons and the Medical Campus to the northeast.

The masterplan created "green windows" into the campus. By opening the campus to the city, rather than creating a distinct edge, the University is able to have a presence within the city. The masterplan creates gateways to the University, and provides density at the interior of the campus. The overall structure of the University pays homage to a typical Quad-oriented configuration, but departs from this model through strategies appropriate to the urban context with increased open space performance.

The first built project of the masterplan was McMicken Commons. The University was in the process of demolishing a temporary building that had been put on the site. A grade change across the site was managed by a series of terraces that made the site difficult to navigate. Hargreaves Associates convinced the University to remove the surface parking lot, and also found that if the terraces were removed, the site could manage a constant four percent slope. By removing the parking and the terraces, the design made the site more accessible, easily traversable,

and contributed to the goal of reducing surface parking. The project created the campus' first major open space and was quickly adopted by the students as the heart of the campus. The success of McMicken Commons lent credibility to the masterplan and transitioned the role of Hargreaves Associates from planners to the designers of the individual landscape spaces.

Over roughly the next fifteen years, the firm would work on a number of open spaces at the University, often corresponding to the development of new major academic buildings. At **The Aronoff Center for Art and Design**, designed by architect Peter Eisenman, Hargreaves Associates designed a series of earthworks that respond to the building's interactions with the site. Eisenman's building slides into the existing slopes of the landscape, and surrounding earthwork landscapes reinforce the action of the building and preserve existing trees.

**UNIVERSITY OF CINCINNATI:
LIBRARY SQUARE**
Cincinnati, Ohio

02

03

Library Square was developed during the construction of the Engineering Research Center, designed by Michael Graves. Library Square serves as a plaza for the Engineering Research Center, the Langsam Library, and Rhodes Hall (an academic building). The plaza also acts as a piece in the chain of continuous open spaces, linking the academic buildings with housing and parking. The design simplifies a grade change that had been previously negotiated with a complex series of ramps and switchbacks responding to each building individually and taking up the entire footprint of the plaza. The new design removes the existing ramps and forms a singular sloped plane so that the buildings share common ground. The plaza is conceived of as an unfurling nautilus, a metaphor for growth – both in the physical form of the plaza and the growth of the mind through the pursuit of knowledge. At the center of the nautilus the Oliver Wendell Holmes quote, "A mind, once stretched by a new idea, never regains its original dimension" is inscribed into the spiral paving. The nautilus form is used in the paving pattern for the plaza playing a strong figurative role viewed from the plazas above, spreading out from the center. As the nautilus unfurls upwards it negotiates the building entrances at different levels.

01-03: The spiraling form of the plaza and its paving pattern references expanding knowledge and the unfolding of space at the multi-level plaza.

UNIVERSITY OF CINCINNATI:
UNIVERSITY COMMONS
Cincinnati, Ohio

01

02

University Commons creates a gateway between the two campuses – the Medical Campus to the northeast and the academic West Campus. The University negotiated a land swap with the city in order to create University Commons, the central open space for the buildings, which include academic, student life buildings, a hotel and conference center and the Vontz Center, a biomedical research center designed by Frank Gehry. Available fill from the excavation that accompanied the new construction prompted a landform-based design that creates verticality with a shifting landscape and corresponds to the undulating forms of the Gehry building. The landforms create both prospect and refuge, rising in height and carving out intimate garden spaces. The gardens within the Commons are especially utilized by the many outside visitors to the conference center.

01,02: The landforms create verticality with a shifting landscape and correspond to the undulating forms of the Gehry center for biomedical research. 03: Aerial view of University Commons. 04: The fountain design references chaos theory. 05: Seating area and place of prospect at the top of the landform.

01

02

03

04

01-04: Movement and form at University Commons

Within the Commons a fountain plaza references the scientific nature of the surrounding buildings, with water movement influenced by chaos theory. The fountain basin is in a gently depressed area, with a curb lip under which water jets emerge and spray random cycles of water from the base. When the fountain is turned off, the dry plaza can be used for special events. Without the flow of water the curb acts as a seatwall that forms an edge of the plaza. At a point of intersection of major roadways with the campus, the landforms act as a vehicular gateway to the University, while at the same time create a sense of enclosure from within the Commons.

01

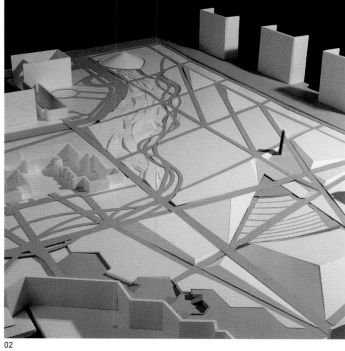

02

UNIVERSITY OF CINCINNATI: CAMPUS GREEN
Cincinnati, Ohio

01: Formerly a seven-acre parking lot, Campus Green forms the primary open and active social space of the campus. **02**: Working scale model. **03.04**: Water, figurative and structural, is incorporated within the system of the paths. **05**: The large landform cone glows red with Euonymus.

03

04

05

The connective, circulation oriented landscape of the academic campus enlarges to form the signature open space of the campus at **Campus Green** and **Sigma Sigma Commons**. Formerly a seven-acre parking lot, Campus Green forms the primary open and active social space of the campus, while still acting as a circulation spine, connecting Main Street with the Medical Campus. Sigma Sigma Commons negotiates a significant grade change between Main Street and Campus Green and takes the form of a series of walkways that prioritize the circulation connection, cutting through and skewing the form of the terraces. The paths "cut stone" through architectonic terraces, orchestrating rough and smooth surfaces to indicate a sense of movement and action of the material. Sigma Sigma Commons also acts as an amphitheater for intimate outdoor classes and larger concerts, performances, and convocations. The angular architectonic planes of Sigma Sigma Commons soften at Campus Green, where a braid of twisting paths and landforms form a landscape of circulation diagonally through the middle of the open space. The circulation braid weaves a strong figure through the center of the Green, allowing for distinct areas for other programmatic needs that cater to the diverse communities of the University – graduate students, undergrads, staff, academic needs of the faculty, large event spaces for large campus events including graduation and alumni events.

UNIVERSITY OF CINCINNATI:
SIGMA SIGMA COMMONS
Cincinnati, Ohio

Foregrounded as landscape figure, the braid emphasizes the connective design goals of the masterplan. The meandering form of the paths references the stream that used to run through Campus Green before the University was established. Water, figurative and structural, is incorporated within the system of the paths. Drainage runs along the braid, returning flowing water along the path. Dynamic fountains along the path also symbolically mark the return of water to the valley. All along the western side of the braid a hilly area of small landforms creates a home for an Arboretum. Hargreaves Associates created a small collection of specimen trees, but left space for additional acquisitions over time, allowing the University to receive trees as gifts from sister universities. The arboretum area allows for space for quiet contemplation, intimate conversation, and study. This type of passive program contrasts with the open lawn on the eastern side of the braid. Here, students play all kinds of informal sports from Frisbee to cricket. This space is also used for tents for alumni and other large University events.

01

02

03

01,02: The paths "cut stone," skewing the form of the architectonic terraces.
03: Sigma Sigma Commons negotiates a significant grade change between Main Street and Campus Green.

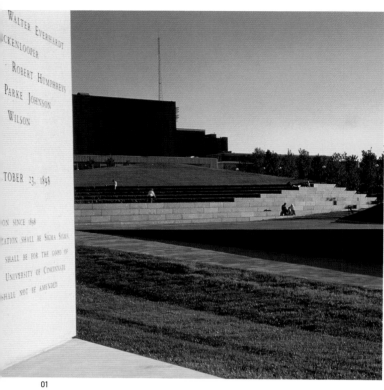

01

02

Small, triangular spaces between the graduate student housing and the larger open play areas are known as Reading Gardens for quiet study, and buffer the graduate students from the more raucous activities of the undergraduates. Reading Gardens to the east of the braid provide additional quiet, small spaces for study and rest. At the Lindner Drive entrance to the University at the northern edge of Campus Green, a large landform cone references the ancient Native American landforms found in the southern Ohio area and marks the entrance to campus. The landform is planted with Euonymus, creating a fiery red, the color of the University.

Within the Campus Green and Sigma Sigma open spaces, the design forms distinct areas of program for the diverse university user groups – undergraduates, graduate students with families, faculty, alumni, and other visitors. By accommodating the varied programs, the space unites the diverse users, making this area a prime social connector of the campus. Sculptural landforms and integrated landscape concepts transcend the typology of the traditional New England Quad. Hargreaves Associates responds to the contemporary urban university with open space with dense and effective program, expanding ideas of university campus planning.

03

UNIVERSITY OF CINCINNATI:
UNIVERSITY PLAZA
Cincinnati, Ohio

A system of gateways throughout the University provides thresholds from the urban fabric to the campus. At **University Plaza** Hargreaves Associates creates a campus entry point through an open plaza. A 120-foot long linear fountain creates a strong visual connection into the campus. The fountain is formed from stone fins that rise from the plaza, spilling water through water spouts into a small pool. This open plaza links the existing campus with the new, as University Plaza introduces the visual language of paving materials from Main Street, the new pedestrian core of the new academic campus, at a key campus entry point. The open space at University Plaza creates a gathering space for University events.

01

02

01-04: The linear fountain at University Plaza is formed from stone fins that rise from the earth.

03

04

UNIVERSITY OF CINCINNATI:
ZIMMER PLAZA
Cincinnati, Ohio

01

Zimmer Plaza, a sculpture garden and circulation connector, is a rooftop plaza that fulfills multiple functions. Once entirely concrete, the plaza is conceived as a "green oasis," an area that is used for passive recreation and study, while at the same time is a key circulation corridor that is highly traveled by students changing classes. The multiple paths through the plaza strengthen the connections between Campus Green and the Academic Ridge at the heart of the campus. The strong geometries of the plaza are echoed in *Forest Devil*, a tensegrity sculpture by Kenneth Snelson that is sited in the plaza, one of the University's designated sculpture gardens. Intimate spaces and lush and varied plantings of flowering trees, perennials and grasses help to create a garden-like atmosphere with seasonal change. The plaza also has open lawns and shaded benches to promote a relaxing environment for study. Constructed on the roof of the Zimmer Auditorium with strict weight limitations, the design concentrates the loading of the trees in the built-up cones at moments of structural support, and implements pedestal paving and green roof technology in order to plant the variety of perennials and trees.

01-02: Zimmer Plaza is a rooftop oasis, sculpture garden, and campus connector.

02

01

02

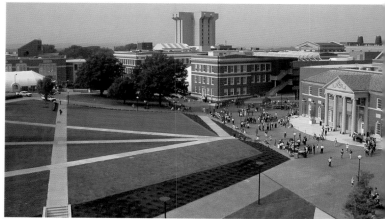

03

UNIVERSITY OF CINCINNATI:
MAIN STREET
Cincinnati, Ohio

Main Street, an intensely programmed connective open space that facilitates a twenty-four hour campus life, is the culminating project for Hargreaves Associates at the University, completed in 2005. The design reinforces the ongoing thematic of connection in the development of the campus, creating a dense urban core at the heart of the University that is academically oriented and pedestrian in nature. The curved geometry of the streetscape influences the geometries of the arced buildings around it including the Morphosis Campus Recreation Center, the Tangeman University Center by Gwathmey Siegel and the Steger Student Life Center by Moore Ruble Yudell Architects & Planners.

04

05

01: Aerial view of Main Street originating from McMicken Commons.
02: Students gather on the stepped seatwalls. **03**: Main Street begins at McMicken Commons. **04**: The curved geometry of the streetscape influences the geometries of the arced buildings around it. **05**: A row of Ginkgo trees follows the arc of Main Street.

These mixed uses, which also include student offices and classrooms, form the core of student life. A distinct hardscape material palette defines the urban character of the circulation spine, creating a strong identity at the core of the urban campus. Broad sloping paved areas and curved granite steps gain access to buildings. Granite outcrops create seatwalls and terraces that make areas for overlooks and gathering for eating and studying, and points of meeting with friends. At Bearcat Plaza, at the entrance of the Tangeman University Center, seating steps fall back from the higher elevation of Main Street. The seat walls descend towards Nippert Stadium, opening up views to the stadium beyond creating a dramatic gathering space along the pedestrian spine, shaded by Lacebark Elm trees. The space is activated at night with lighting. At the north, columnar trees transition the urban hardscape to the lush plantings and open lawns of Campus Green.

01

02

03

01: Granite steps and seatwall at Bearcat Plaza. 02: Ginkgo trees line Main Street. 03: Looking towards Main Street from Bearcat Plaza. 04: The design creates a dense urban core at the heart of the University that is academically oriented and pedestrian in nature. 05: Bearcat Plaza creates a dramatic gathering space with views to Nippert Stadium beyond.

04

05

01

01: Seating steps fall at Bearcat Plaza fall back from the higher
elevation of Main Street. 02: The signature open space exemplifies
the masterplan goal for an activated, twenty-four hour campus.
03: Broad sloping paved areas and curved granite steps form
a distinct hardscape material palette creating a strong identity
at the core of the urban campus.

As the culmination of the University of Cincinnati Masterplan, Main Street reverses the academic typology of academic buildings forming the urban edge with protected open quads at the interior. Rather, the edges of the University of Cincinnati campus are open, inviting flows into the center, and creating density at the interior. Main Street creates a pedestrian, academic urban core that is focused entirely on student life with open access to the Student Life Center and Recreation Center. Hargreaves Associates spent over fifteen years at the University of Cincinnati, working closely with University officials to craft a thriving campus, shaping the masterplan and the built campus over time. As each new open space project was implemented, new possibilities emerged for the academic and student life goals of the University. In an ongoing dialogue between the designers and the University, the masterplan evolved through guidelines into built form, creating a thriving contemporary campus.

02

03

01

01: Behind Main Street folded landforms merge with the Morphosis Campus Recreation Center. 02: Main Street forms the heart of the twenty-four hour campus. 03: In an ongoing dialogue over fifteen years, the masterplan evolved through guidelines into built form, creating a thriving contemporary campus.

02

03

01

02

03

SYDNEY OLYMPICS 2000
Sydney, Australia

At **Sydney Olympics 2000**, Hargreaves Associates created an open space of heroic scale with a sense of sweeping majesty of large scale plazas while remaining responsive to the human scale experience of public space. The firm's involvement began with developing a comprehensive masterplan that would unite existing disparate plans for various Olympic stadiums and venues. With the masterplan, a systematic site strategy addresses the practical issues of accommodating the huge amounts of visitors to the site during the games, as well as infrastructural issues of water management and environmental remediation, all while creating a generous, iconic landscape appropriate to the grandness of the Olympics. The site design is developed through a three-tiered approach – *Red Moves, Blue Moves*, and *Green Moves* – that guide, respectively, circulation, water, and vegetation. These three systems work together to create an integrated landscape experience for the Games that is rooted in the specifics of the site as a post-industrial landscape, polluted through 19th century industrial activities as an abattoir.

01: The large scale plaza creates an open space of heroic scale with a sense of sweeping majesty for the Olympic Games. **02.03**: The centralized Olympic Plaza can accommodate up to 500,000 visitors a day.

01

02

The *Red Move* addresses urban space – circulation and the overall site arrangements. The Olympic venue would receive a massive influx of visitors during the Games, and had to have the capacity to accommodate them. The *Red Move* creates a plaza concept for the site, unifying all of the Olympic venues by creating one, centralized Olympic Plaza that could accommodate up to 500,000 visitors a day and that each of the individual stadiums and smaller plazas could clip on to. Each of the major venues – the Olympic Stadium, the Aquatic Center, and the Arena – are joined by the large plaza that acts as an enlarged boulevard, providing access for all. The large plaza links directly to the transportation center that brings visitors to the site, leading the visitors directly to the main circulation thoroughfare. The geometries of the footprints of the former abattoirs overlaid onto the boulevard plaza create the dynamic paving pattern of the plaza. The firm worked with manufacturers of permeable pavers to create a range of hues in red and ochre that recall the Australian desert. Water is harvested from the entire site including all rooftops and ground surfaces. The porous paving is a key component of collecting the stormwater on site, which is treated in the wetlands and recycled through the site. Tree-lined edges and lighting pylons with solar canopies offer shade, shelter and illumination throughout the plaza.

01: The design remains responsive to the human scale experience of public space. 02: The plaza at the Olympic Stadium forms a generous, iconic landscape. 03: During the heat of the Games, the *Fig Grove* became a popular meeting spot, an area of relaxation away from the main sporting events. 04: The *Red Move* clips the individual sporting venues on to one unifying Olympic Plaza.

03

04

01

01: At the Fig Grove Fountains bridgeways allow visitors to be immersed in the fountain, or stay dry if they wish.
02: At the Northern Water Feature steel cones spray arches of water across the stepped pool.

01

02

03

The *Blue Move* introduces designed water features to the Olympic Complex. Conceptually, Hargreaves Associates sought to create major water features at the high point and low points of the site. The Fig Grove is at the high point of the site and forms the crossroads as the point of arrival of the transportation system. This interactive space uses water in fountains to immediately engage visitors as they arrive to the Games. Intersecting and overlapping bridgeways allow visitors to be immersed in the fountain, or stay dry if they wish. Large fig trees with canopies 160' in diameter provide a leafy respite. During the heat of the Games, the Fig Grove became a popular meeting spot, an area of relaxation away from the main sporting events.

01-03: The fountain at the Northern Water Feature creates dramatic endpoint to the Olympic Plaza.

01

02

03

04

01: Fountains at the Northern Water Feature aerate collected runoff from the site. 02: The large pyramidal mound for climbing also entombs the hazardous soil that was found on the site. 03: Children play in the fountains. 04: A layered approach of the site – water, circulation and vegetation – creates a rich landscape.

The second fountain is located at the low point of the site at the end of the long Olympic Plaza. This fountain uses water collected from across the entire catchment area of the site. Lines of steel cones spray a growing arch of water over three tiers, from the raised plaza and descending by stepped seatwalls into a pool above the Northern Water Feature. While aesthetically providing a dramatic endpoint to the plaza boulevard, the fountain also works in concert with the treatment wetland, aerating the collected water. The Northern Water Feature treats the 260 acre catchment of Homebush Bay, including all Olympic arenas, plazas, and buildings. The collected stormwater from Homebush drains conventionally underground and then outfalls into the wetland, which has a meandering, though clearly constructed, shape, dropping gradually in elevation, retaining the water of a twenty year storm event for two days. The banks of the wetland are tiered at increments in order to support specific wetland species. Once the clean water reaches the end of the wetland sequence it is pumped into storage locations that feed the on-site water fountains and irrigation systems, or if the storage facilities are full, the water returns to an existing creek. In this way, the design is able to systematically incorporate sustainability into the infrastructure of the site, as well as having the infrastructural and cleaning systems become a public amenity. At the end of the boulevard, a pier extends over the Northern Water Feature allowing visitors to engage with the wetland and to look back onto the Olympic venues. Another consequence of the huge environmental cleanup, a large pyramidal mound next to the wetland entombs the hazardous soil that was found on the site. Hargreaves Associates converted this large structure into a climbing mound, transforming waste into an amenity and providing a scenic overlook to the Olympic Site, a popular gathering place at each sunset during the Games.

01

01: The Northern Water Feature treats the 260-acre catchment of Homebush Bay, including all Olympic arenas, plazas, and buildings. 02: Diagram showing the collection, treatment, and circulation of water. 03: The Northern Water Feature has a meandering, though clearly constructed, shape. 04: A pier extends over the Northern Water Feature allowing visitors to engage with the wetland and to look back onto the Olympic venues. 05: A legacy for Australia, the Olympic Park continues to be used for aquatic and other sports events.

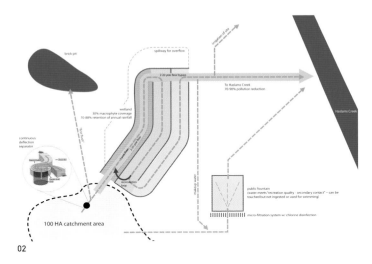

02

03

04

05

The *Green Moves* of the project describe vegetation strategy – five east/west green "fingers" of trees, creating richly vegetated corridors that link the urban core of the Olympic venues with the surrounding Millennium Park. Other vegetation strategies implemented include the use of permeable paving and structural soils to support the trees in the paved areas, including the large fig trees in the Olympic Plaza that were transported to the site via barge. The fig trees in the Fig Grove were salvaged from the site. Because of their large size, with the trees measuring over 160' in diameter, the transplant process took a full year to accomplish.

The Hargreaves Associates design for the Sydney Olympics 2000 harnessed a major world event to create a park that would succeed as a showcase for Australia to present itself to the world, as well as a park that continues to be used long after the signature event is over. The site continues to be used as a leisure and sporting facility, with much activity centered on the Aquatic Center. The vastness of the scale of the space acts as a memorial to the past event that took place there. The Olympics project also was the impetus to transform a brownfield site, cleaning a polluted site and transferring it into the public domain. The firm used sustainable technology to clean water on site and create long-term structures that allow the plant material to thrive and for the park structures to perform into the future. The space is a legacy for Australia and Sydney.

WILLIAM J. CLINTON PRESIDENTIAL
CENTER PARK
Little Rock, Arkansas

The **William J Clinton Presidential Center Park**, sites the
Clinton Presidential Center and provides a legacy of open public
space in Little Rock. The park bridges the national with the local,
transitioning between the narrative of the Clinton presidency
that is portrayed from within the Center, with the immediate
geographic and cultural conditions of the Arkansas River and
downtown Little Rock. The central downtown waterfront park
provides a place where local residents can spend time by the
river, fishing, barbequing, and relaxing. In this, the park facilitates
a narrative of American democracy that joins the iconic with
the everyday

01: The site framework overlays the city grids – one oriented to the
River and the other to the national Jeffersonian grid. 02: The Boulevard
approaches the Presidential Center.

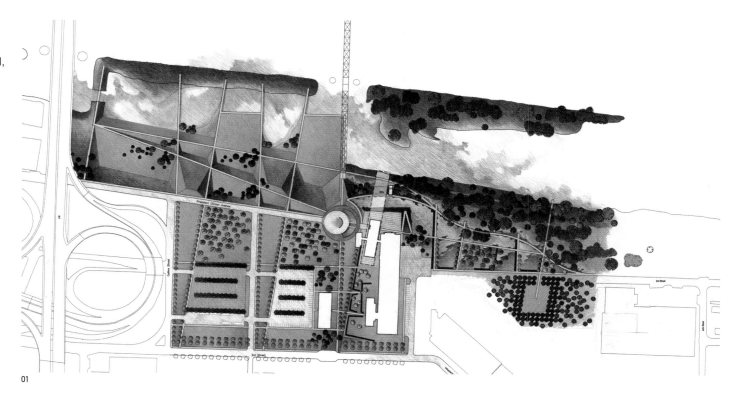

01

02

01

Hargreaves Associates collaborated with Polshek Partnership, the architects for the building, to site the structure and develop the landscape as a "bridge to the 21st Century," reinforcing the architectural concept for the Center. The metaphor of the bridge manifests itself in the landscape through ideas of connection – making connections between the site and its context to downtown Little Rock and the Arkansas River for the overall site organization and to connect people to this context. Located on 30 acres on the banks of the Arkansas River in Little Rock on a former light industrial site, the site facilitates the typical uses of a public park, coexisting with landscape program that supports the Presidential Center. Facilitating connections with the Arkansas River, the park restructures the edge condition, which was previously cut off with a 45' steep bluff. The design grades back the land with folding earthworks in order to make it usable with more gentle slopes. Program is nested within the folds of the earthworks – the Amphitheater that seats up to 2000 people, and the future Children's Playground.

01: Folded topography restructures the edge to the Arkansas River.
02-05: The site structure situates the architecture, which rests in easy dialog with the landscape of folded topograpy.

02

03

04

05

06

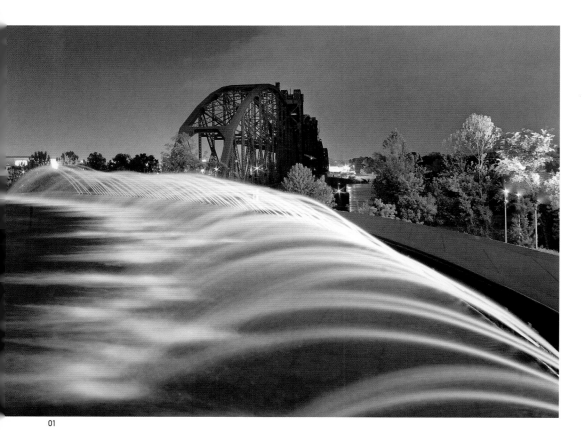

Formulating a way to structure the new landscape and reinforce the connections to the urban fabric, Hargreaves Associates developed a site strategy that overlays the two competing city grids of Little Rock, one oriented to the Arkansas River, the other to the national Jeffersonian grid. The resulting framework guides the rationale for situating the library, which rests in easy dialog with the landscape, as well as the other landscape spaces, creating zones for program oriented landscape typologies. The site framework allows for transitions between programs associated directly with the library, with recreation program for the waterfront park. The continuation of the street grid provides the structure of the park's circulation, marked with paths and steps that connect to the various program elements within the park.

01-02: The fountain sprays arcs of jumping water, celebrating the entrance to the Presidential Center.

01

02

01

02

The Presidential Center is located at the center of the park, with landscape program radiating outwards from the building. The Celebration Circle and Fountain form a central node that guides the approach to the Library facility. As a dramatic front door to the Library, the plaza and fountain create a strong identity for the Presidential Center. The fountain sprays arcs of jumping water, celebrating the entrance to the Center. In quieter moments, the fountain forms an elegant pool reflecting the architecture and sky. Embedded within the park are programmed areas both flexible and more structured for the range of events hosted by the Center. The Scholars' Garden is adjacent to the Presidential Center building and has three garden rooms, each defined by low walls, hedges, and garden furniture. These gardens provide space for lunches and informal meetings for the employees of the Archives as well as small, organized events. The East Lobby Terrace is able to host small events and looks on to the Arkansas Forest and the Riparian Bank.

01-02: The folded landforms bridge connections from the river to the architecture.

01

02

03

04

05

01.02: The Scholars' Garden provides space for informal meetings and small organized events. 03: The downtown park provides a place where local residents can spend relaxing time by the river. 04: The Scholars' Garden next to the Library. 05: The Celebration Circle and Fountain form a central node that guides the approach to the Library facility.

Adjacent to the riverbank, the slope to the river is gentle and is maintained as a naturalized East Riparian Bank and Meadow, showcasing native trees, grasses and wildflowers. A meandering pathway negotiates the riparian edge, connecting the lower banks with the Amphitheater. The larger vegetation strategy employs plants native to Arkansas, highlighting the local at this national destination. The Arkansas Forest area of the site creates an arboretum of trees found in the Ozark and Ouachita Mountain Regions of Arkansas, as well as other trees specific to the West Gulf Coastal Plain and the Delta Region. The East Revetment area is kept in its current condition, with local ecology groups studying its ecological systems and working to maintain and improve the area for wildlife habitat. Beyond the Riparian Banks a Contemplation Grove creates an informal outdoor room for quiet meditation, and creates a solemn environment for a future chapel that will be built in this area.

01

01: The fountain creates a strong identity for the Presidential Center.
02-03: Low walls, hedges, and garden furniture define the outdoor rooms of the Scholars' Garden.

02

03

01

Unlike other waterfront parks, the focus of this park is aimed, in part, away from the river and toward the Presidential Center as a national symbol of *Democracy*. The park incorporates the Arkansas River into the design concept and form, but the focus shifts toward access and a more quotidian notion of a *democratic* use of space for the citizenry. The Park is further able to facilitate the shifts between the "big D" *Democratic* symbolic presentation of space and the "small d" *democratic* use of space through a systematic and comprehensive approach to program. Through concise and separate landscape typologies the park unifies the mission of the Center, portraying a national presidency, with the local reality of a dynamic river ecology and the needs of the local residents.

02

01-02: Next to the Arkansas River a Contemplation Grove creates an informal outdoor room for quiet meditation.

01

02

MARKINGS - REVELATORY LANDSCAPES
San José, California

The work of Hargreaves Associates has looked to contemporary art practice in several ways. In early projects, looking to the earthworks artists provided precedent and techniques that allowed the firm to break out of modernist, composition oriented design. At Candlestick Park and Byxbee Park, collaborations with environmental artists helped dictate design strategies emphasizing a phenomenological reading of landscape. In projects since then, the firm has often worked closely with artists to site public art within larger projects. Landscape architects also present their work through institutional museum spaces. The firm participated in Groundswell, the 2005 Museum of Modern Art exhibition that was only the second exhibition of landscape architecture at the Museum. The garden festival is another type of exhibition that presents concepts of landscape architecture to the public.
In 1996, the firm created an installation at the garden festival at Chaumont-sur-Loire in France, using the design principles of the firm in the creation of a small garden.

03

In a hybrid of all of these modes of practice and display, Hargreaves Associates participated in the 2001 San Francisco Museum of Modern Art (SFMOMA) exhibition, *Revelatory Landscapes*, organized by international design curator Aaron Betsky. Here, the firm created **Markings**, a temporary installation that was among five different projects sited in the Bay Area, each a collaboration between a landscape architect and an artist. The exhibition explored how landscape architects generate design from site, revealing the landscape and its cultural and environmental forces, rather than obscuring site with a superimposed design. In choosing locations for their projects all of the firms showed how landscape architects were in the process of staking out new territories for the profession. Landscape architects were reiterating their claim to make place in peripheral spaces – the derelict, left-over, forgotten spaces at the edges of developed built fabric.

Hargreaves Associates chose a site in San José, California, at the head of Guadalupe River Park, on the underside of a massive junction of highway overpasses. A forest of concrete pylons supports the highway overhead. Though the site is surrendered to infrastructure, on the forgotten side of the highway, it is also located alongside the Guadalupe River, and a historical site as a former encampment of the Chochenyo Native Americans in the 18th and 19th centuries. At the time of the exhibition San José was undergoing massive transformation as the capitol of Silicon Valley. The firm had already explored these intriguing social conditions in their earlier work at Plaza de César Chávez and Guadalupe River Park.

Hargreaves Associates teamed with Native American poet Julian Lang to create an installation that could draw out and reference this complex collision of history, infrastructure, nature and culture. The design team employed two simple operations, painting the concrete pylons silver and creating a linear earthen berm directly under a slot in the highway ramps above. Visitors that climbed the earthwork could gain prospect on the installation and feel a larger part of the expanded spatial relationships.

01: The firm teamed with Native American poet Julian Lang to create an art installation at the Guadalupe River in San José. 02: The installation revealed the complex collisions of history, infrastructure, nature and culture that give shape to our contemporary landscape. 03: The linear earthen berm under the highway allowed participants to experience expanded spatial relationships.

01

02

03

04

The silver columns acted to bring light into the underpass and to highlight the column's form and power of space making. The silver columns echo the linear form of the highways overhead and the adjacent Guadalupe River. Lang devised a series of words, in English and Karuk (the indigenous Native American language) that are inscribed on the columns. The illuminated forest of inscribed columns created a sense of place at the misbegotten location. The words chosen – *path, earth, sky, together* – exposed and united the layers of human culture on the site – the Native American past, the Anglo highway infrastructure, and the ongoing natural system of the Guadalupe River.

The installation transformed a derelict overpass into a marked place of awakening, revealing the substance and materials of landscape architecture – the complex relationships between natural systems and human inhabitation. These relationships form the essence of how Hargreaves Associates practices in larger, more complex park projects increasingly sited on brownfield sites. With the installation, the firm used the techniques and language of an art practice to shed light onto the design practice of the firm, creating space and meaning through minimal yet powerful intervention. By exposing the latent conditions of this particular site, the installation was able to suggest a larger implication – that there is content in all of our forgotten, left-over landscapes, and all of these landscapes have the power to affirm the connections between nature and all peoples.

01-04: The words chosen expose and unite the layers of human culture on the site – the Native American past, the Anglo highway infrastructure, and the ongoing natural system of the Guadalupe River.

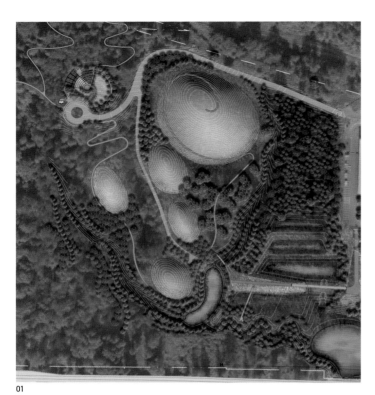

01

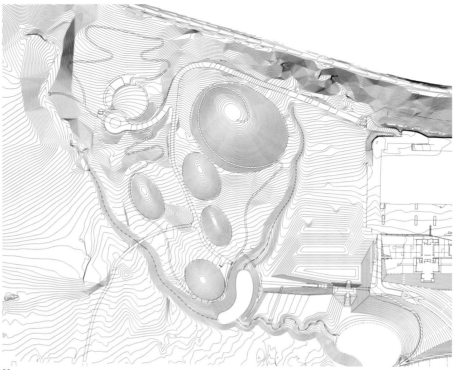

02

03

BRIGHTWATER MITIGATION AREA
Snohomish County, Washington

04

01: The Northern Mitigation Area restores wetland and habitat adjacent to a waste water treatment plant in Washington. 02: The grading of the site is designed in order for the water to flow from the high point to the low point, creating the four distinct habitats. 03: Only the precise flow of water allows for the habitat to be restored and maintained. 04: Aerial view.

At **Brightwater**, Hargreaves Associates constructs a landscape for a waste treatment plant in Snohomish County, Washington State. When operable, the facility will clean fifty-two million gallons of water a day. The landscape is divided into three areas – ninety acres that sites the main industrial treatment facility, the Northern Mitigation Area, forty acres adjacent to the treatment facility that restores wetland and habitat to the area, and an off-site pump station. Through a didactic representation of how water flows through an ecological system, Brightwater creates a powerful landscape of display.

At the Northern Mitigation Area, the design creates a landscape of display while at the same time facilitating a massive environmental remediation and ecological restoration. The land of the Northern Mitigation Area had been polluted over the

decades of industrial use. Large piles of debris, invasive reeds, felled trees and broken glass filled creeks that were originally on the site, as well as a fish rearing pond connected to the creek. The design first provides operations that clean the site and then creates a landscape that restores four degrees of habitat - fish rearing pond, emergent wetlands, wet meadows, and upland meadows. Each of these habitat areas is calibrated to meet stringent environmental federal and state standards for soils, water flow and habitat.

Controlling and managing the water flows is the key criteria to create independently functioning ecological habitat regions. The grading of the site is designed in order for the water to flow from the high point to the low point, facilitating the creation of four distinct habitats.

01

02

03

UNCOMMON PLACES: BRIGHTWATER MITIGATION AREA

Only the precise flow of water allows for the habitat to be restored and maintained. Key to controlling the flow of water is creating soil profiles that produce the correct levels of water retention as water flows through the site. Original soil conditions lacked organic content and were unable to retain water. Hargreaves Associates found a way to kick start the carbon cycle on the site which contained almost no topsoil by using a thick mantle of compost from the mulch of non-native trees found on site.

In order for the public to have access to this delicate ecological restoration, the design incorporates a trail system with bridges and overlooks that runs through the site, allowing for recreation without disturbance. The Northern Mitigation Area is a restoration of habitat, with minimal human occupation. Educational uses of the site are encouraged by the trail, with docents from the wastewater facility giving talks about the creation of a habitat, plant succession and ecological education. There are classroom and lab facilities for students to learn and make ecological experiments. The County also sponsors an art studio on the site to have visiting artists interact with the functions of the plant to clean water and support ecological habitat.

At the Main Plant facility a foregrounded landscape of folded earthworks treats stormwater on the site in a public landscape that is explored through trails, boardwalks and overlooks. As the landforms provide terrain to be experienced and facilitate the movement and cleansing of stormwater, they also function by concealing the industrial treatment facility from the surrounding landscape and community. Within the landforms a comprehensive stormwater management strategy funnels, retains, and treats all stormwater (from the roofs and ground surfaces) on site through a system of ponds and dams. Ultimately the stormwater is released, clean, into the adjacent Little Bear Creek. A linear channel that is the first stage of the cleaning process also acts as a barrier to the secure aspects of the treatment facility, providing another buffer from public to private. A system of pathways leads public visitors through the large, interlocking landforms with varying emergent wetland conditions and plant communities.

At Brightwater, Hargreaves Associates creates a landscape that balances seemingly contradictory goals and ideas. The design implements a technical process to artificially create a natural landscape. Brightwater is a landscape of display alongside a landscape of concealment. The landscape demonstrates and provides direct access to ecological processes while facilitating vital civic services of waste water treatment. These contradictions create a richly nuanced project within a large scale landscape that is simultaneously gestural and precise.

Uncommon Places are extraordinary landscapes borne from extraordinary sites. The projects of *Uncommon Places* work to articulate the variety of landscape experience and the continuum of methods, tools and expressions of place-making. The landscapes of *Uncommon Places* define site as physical place, as cultural condition, and as mode of practice, all enhancing an understanding of the ever expanding boundaries of landscape architecture. In these projects, Hargreaves Associates takes up the work that they initiated in the first days of their practice, breaking beyond over-simplified modernist tabula rasa constructions of space. *Uncommon Places* articulate complex relationships between nature and culture, ecology and history. Through these projects, the firm explores the process, the subject, the object and the field, always working the boundaries of landscape architectural practice.

01-06: A trail system with bridges and overlooks runs through the site, allowing for recreation without disturbance of the delicate ecologies.

04

05

06

SMALLER

MINNEAPOLIS RESIDENCE
Minneapolis, Minnesota

01

02

While Hargreaves Associates is primarily known for the design of urban parks and large waterfronts, the firm has simultaneously pursued smaller projects that call for different design approaches and strategies. These projects look to the smaller site and its unique requirements as an integral part of their complete practice. The site conditions of smaller projects demand design strategies appropriate to the scale, focusing on potent design narratives, the systematic organization of space, and a fine grain of detail. Where the firm's large scale projects often harness interactions with natural processes, the smaller scale projects are inherently less process-oriented. At the large scale site the starting point of the design is often clear, with visible cultural and ecological impacts developed over a long period of time. On a smaller site, these larger impacts often do not register as indelibly. In these projects, it is vital to present an unambiguous design strategy and an integrated, clarified set of forms that express the strategy. Beyond the program given by the client, and the needs of the eventual users, Hargreaves Associates seeks a compelling design image that drives the project toward the elucidation of a fully developed concept.

At the **Minneapolis Residence**, a private home in Minnesota, the foundation of the design is the collection of modern sculpture owned by the clients and their desire for a true collaboration between art, architecture and landscape. Hargreaves Associates worked closely with Vincent James Architects in an evolving process that developed an elegant choreography of the landscape, art and architecture, shifting in relationship to each other. While the landscape works hand-in-hand with the architecture, it also performs as a distinct landscape separate from the house. Volumetric outdoor rooms flow one to the next, creating a series of galleries to site the contemporary sculpture collection and a landscape for strolling outside of the art experience.

03

04

01.02: A collection of modern sculpture forms the basis of a true collaboration between art, architecture and landscape. **03:** Floor to ceiling windows frame views and incorporate the landscape as a picture plane within the house. **04:** In the landscape the art is foregrounded by precise volumetric spaces.

The underlying geometry of the plan arrangement creates a structure that begins the work of unifying art, landscape and architecture. Though the plan has the appearance of an ordered, modernist pavilion / courtyard, the overall experience of the space facilitates dynamic motion. The concept for the experience of the space is of a "crystalline box," where the volumes and surfaces seem to "sparkle" as you move through them, merging spatial movement with the visual[1]. This movement activates shifting relationships where landscape, art and architecture are alternately object and field, figure and ground. These mutable relationships are achieved through several tangible design strategies.

Floor to ceiling windows frame views of landscape and art from the interior, incorporating the landscape as a picture plane within the house. The building structure disappears at the corners of these windows, further breaking down traditional architecture and encouraging views to the lake to the southwest. At the same time, matching interior and exterior floor elevations create a continuous groundplane between inside and outside. Architectural walls extend into the landscape, and the roof planes merge the architecture with the landscape.

01

02

01: While appearing orthogonal, the lawn has a lens shape that brings the eye to the view of the lakes. **02:** The outdoor rooms order movement and the experience of viewing the works of art in the landscape. **03:** In plan, the elliptical lawn diverges from the underlying geometry of the architecture, but on site it reinforces the overall spatial experience. **04:** A series of rippling landforms forms another distinct room.

The sculpture collection consists of both indoor and outdoor works. Visual links from the interior to exterior sculptures emphasize elegant transitions across thresholds. The architecture allows for easy access to the exterior, so that movement between the interior and exterior sculptures flows freely. At alternating moments, the art, architecture and landscape are contained within a composition, and at other moments each is engaged through movement. In this way, there is a sophisticated balance between motion and pause, action and stillness.

In the landscape the art is foregrounded by precise volumetric spaces, outdoor rooms that order movement and the experience of viewing the works of art in the landscape. The design sculpts a terraced lawn that provides an open space along the slope, with a retaining wall on the downside toward the lakes. Works of art by Richard Serra and Scott Burton inhabit the lawn. While appearing orthogonal, the lawn has a lens shape that brings the eye to the view of the lakes. In plan, the elliptical lawn diverges from the underlying geometry of the architecture, but on the site it reinforces the overall spatial experience, emphasizing the phenomenological experience of designed landscape interacting with architecture and the borrowed nature of the lakes over any formalist diagram. To keep the spare integrity of the lawn, the design avoids a guardrail by creating a kind of inverted ha-ha, cutting down three feet on the edge of the lawn, and filling that space with shrubs that are kept trimmed to the level of the lawn, providing an invisible barrier. A series of rippling landforms forms another distinct room and creates an activated ground for the dynamic sculptures of David Nash. A restrained terrace with stone seatwalls and an elevated grove of honey locusts forms another volume and a setting for sculpture by Elsworth Kelly. The subtleties of the site are integrated into shifting volumetric spaces that create movement through the site, seamlessly negotiating landscape, art and architecture. The project succeeds by activating the viewer, creating a dynamic experience of subject, object and field.

02

03

01: A restrained terrace with stone seatwalls and an elevated grove of honey locusts provides a setting for sculpture by Elsworth Kelly. 02: A Richard Serra sculpture on the elliptical lawn. 03: The landscape creates an activated ground for the dynamic sculptures of David Nash.

NATIONAL MUSEUM OF EMERGING SCIENCE AND INNOVATION
Tokyo, Japan

01

The **Museum of Emerging Science and Innovation** in Tokyo takes its cues from the program of the institution and the deeply embedded cultural history of Japan. The design of the site expresses the union of the culture of research and innovation in science with Japanese traditions. At the outset of the project, the client took the design team on a tour of Zen gardens throughout Japan, framing the project within the ancient landscape traditions of the country. In the museum landscape the design seeks to fuse the formal language of the Zen garden with the contemporary language of science through a series of plazas and gardens. Each of the landscapes of the museum plays with the forms of science, expressions of light, sound and wavelengths, and the materials, textures and overall forms of the Japanese gardens. The synthesized spaces that result place the content of the museum – emerging science and innovation – within a broader cultural narrative.

01: The design of the site expresses the union of research and innovation in science with cultural traditions. 02: The materials of Japanese gardens are fused with the forms of science. 03: Sculptural landforms partially submerged in water express the collision and fusion of molecules.

02

The landscape program – urban plaza, exhibition area, and a central promenade – supports the architecture of the museum and facilitates the education and performance display requirements of the museum. The spaces are finely detailed with a rich material palette appropriate to the civic nature of the facility. Traditional Japanese black river-washed stone contrasts with industrially cut granite in bold bands that pattern the surface of the plaza. A grove of bamboo shades the plaza where seating is provided for the visitors. In the entry plaza to the museum, borrowing both from Zen gardens and the culture of science, sculptural landforms partially submerged in water express the collision and fusion of molecules. In the exhibition area, undulating landforms also combine the forms of Zen gardens with wavelengths of light and sound. In this area, the architecture of the building opens to the landscape, allowing for the possibility of extending the interior exhibitions outside.

01: The synthesized spaces that result place the content of the museum within a broader cultural narrative. **02.03:** The building opens to the landscape, allowing for the possibility of extending the interior exhibitions outside.

01: The landscape program facilitates the education and performance display requirements of the museum. **02**: Traditional Japanese black river-washed stone contrasts with industrially cut granite in bold bands that pattern the surface of the plaza. **03**: The design crafts the forms of science, expressions of light, sound, and wavelengths through materiality and textures.

01

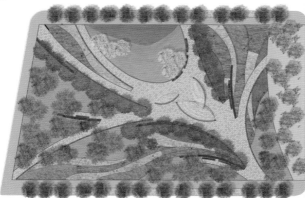

02

03

BELO GARDENS
Dallas, Texas

Belo Gardens was developed as one of three high priority downtown park opportunities identified by Hargreaves Associates working with Carter & Burgess, in their 2003 Downtown Parks Masterplan for the city of Dallas. The goal of the masterplan is to enhance the character of the city through the introduction of a park network and thereby encourage a return of economic investment to downtown Dallas. Without the opportunity for one large downtown park, the masterplan identifies many sites around the city that could be converted into parks, and three high priority sites at critical roadway entrances to the city. The system of parks act as a gateway into the city and express a range of activity, collectively acting to serve the open space needs of the city. The Belo Gardens site was identified as a garden park, balanced with the other parks that feature more civic and heavily programmed urban parks. Belo Corp, one of the primary clients for the Open Space Masterplan, agreed to finance the construction of one of the parks – Belo Gardens. After construction, the park will be owned and maintained by the City of Dallas. In a location that will serve as an informal gateway to Dallas, Belo Gardens is crafted as a high-quality shady retreat with passive recreation, providing a garden oasis for Dallas.

The design approach at Belo Gardens balances the idea of the park as a welcoming garden experience with civic and urban qualities. The structure of the park is oriented internally, with curving paths through gardens leading to a central fountain plaza. This approach creates an interior garden environment with strong visual connections to the streetscape to draw passers by from the street into the heart of the park. The overall design language of the park is derived from abstracted tree forms. On the ground this takes the form of paths branching like tree limbs, separating a series of gardens and groves. The shallow curve of the paving pattern contributes to a rich sense of materiality, reinforced by granite surfaces, hardwood benches and unique lighting. At the central plaza, the interactive fountain also references the language of trees, with the fountain water creating three-dimensional arced leaf shapes. A single grassy

01: Belo Gardens is crafted as a high-quality shady retreat with passive recreation, providing a garden oasis for Dallas. 02: The overall design language of the park is derived from abstracted tree forms. 03: The lighting of the park reinforces the design. 04: The park will serve as an informal gateway to Dallas. 05: The structure of the park is oriented internally, with curving paths through gardens leading to a central fountain plaza.

04

landform mound contains the central plaza space creating enclosure and a sunny play surface for children. A twelve-foot granite wall forms the eastern border of the site, staging a textured backdrop for an area of moveable tables and chairs. This area creates an area of flexible program suitable to the urban setting.

The horticultural aspects of the park are important to the overall design and work by integrating native plants of Texas with decorative grasses and local horticultural traditions. Planting is arranged in long, sweeping drifts that relate to the branching paths. The plantings enclose the fountain plaza and the garden plaza, emphasizing the sense of enclosure of the garden. A layer of taller trees provide shade and a zone of smaller flowering trees create color and texture nearer to the groundplane. The systematic planting of trees works with the shrubs and perennials to create a rich textured environment. A civic garden, the experience at the park favors a quiet exploration and respite from the city.

05

SHAW CENTER FOR THE ARTS
Baton Rouge, Louisiana

The **Shaw Center for the Arts**, a complex of arts institutions in downtown Baton Rouge, is located on a three-acre site across from the Old State Capitol, with views to the Mississippi River. Hargreaves Associates designed a plaza for the Center that provides a unified space for its arts institutions – The LSU Museum of Art, the Manship Theater, two Black Box theaters, the Brunner Gallery contemporary arts space, and the LSU School of Art Gallery. Hargreaves Associates worked closely with the architects, Eskew+Dumez+Ripple and Schwartz/ Silver Architects, to create a civic identity for the unusual institutional hybrid.

01: The Shaw Center is a unified civic plaza with a unique identity for an unusual institutional hybrid of several arts institutions. **02**: The shifting dynamic geometries of the landscape unifies the new architecture with the surrounding plaza and streetscape. **03**: The landscape works closely with the new architecture of the asymmetrical built forms of the new and existing buildings.

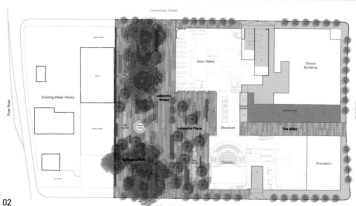

The landscape unifies the new architecture with the surrounding plaza and streetscape, enhancing the visual identity of the architecture. The architecture and landscape were developed together and reference the barge traffic on the nearby Mississippi River through shifting dynamic geometries. In the architecture, this is echoed in the composition of the asymmetrical built forms of the new and existing buildings. Using a strategy derived from Jazz, the design conceives of the plaza as different strands of rhythms, melodies and harmonies that could perform on their own, and then reunite. This pattern of syncopation – short, fat, thin and long dashed – evolved into a paving pattern that equally references the Mississippi River, its barge traffic and its ever-changing meandering river flows. The Mississippi River is reinforced through the presence of water on the site. Two interactive fountains at either end of the plaza create a dialogue with each other and create an immersive environment, masking street noise and engaging visitors to the Center.

02   03

01.02: A syncopated paving pattern references the barge traffic of the Mississippi River and its ever-changing meandering river flows.
03: The river is reinforced through the presence of water on the site.

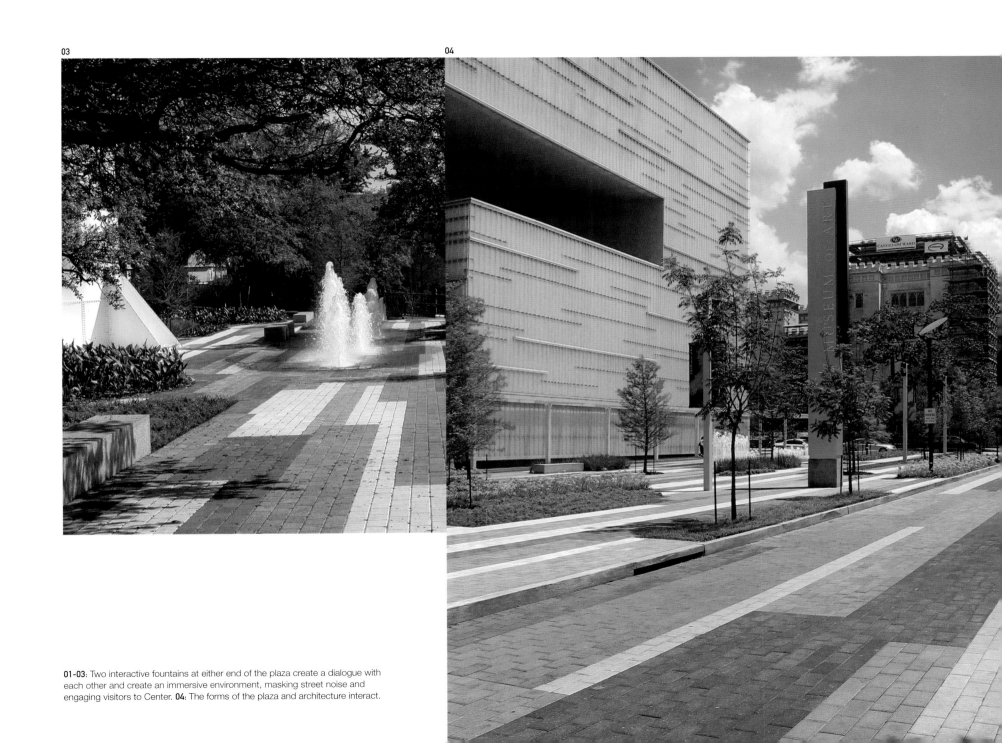

03

04

01-03: Two interactive fountains at either end of the plaza create a dialogue with each other and create an immersive environment, masking street noise and engaging visitors to Center. 04: The forms of the plaza and architecture interact.

The paving pattern creates a unified plaza and extends across the street, enlarging the footprint of the project and situating the Shaw Center within a larger urban context. A through street, Lafayette Street, is incorporated within the total design through the continuation of the paving pattern across the street. The Center can choose to close the street off during special events, or leave it open, maintaining vehicular through access.

Included in the design of the Shaw Center is the renovation of the existing Lafayette Park. The park is completely integrated within the civic space of the Plaza. A line of heritage Live Oak trees that was a part of the old park was preserved and incorporated into the design. Newly planted Bald Cypress trees drift through the plaza and contrast with the older stately trees. The planting palette takes a few of the classic elements of a Deep South garden and configures them in an unfamiliar way, allocating a single species to each lengthy, but narrow, interlocking rectangular bed. A lawn covers a single slope that extends toward the river and offers a counterpoint to the paved expanse. A major component of the revitalization of downtown, the project became a catalyst for other improvements in the district, with restaurants opening near the plaza, new construction of residential buildings and the renovation of an adjacent hotel.

01.02: Heritage Live Oak trees that were a part of the old park are preserved and incorporated into the design.

ONE ISLAND EAST
Hong Kong, China

The design for **One Island East** in Hong Kong creates an urban plaza that bridges the competing open space and circulation needs of a commercial office tower with 15,000 workers with adjacent high density residential housing of 50,000 residents. Hargreaves Associates created a flexible program that provides a range of open space within the landscape. A plaza with artesian fountain at the base of the new office tower serves the business needs of the commercial tower, and a park-like setting with cascade fountains provides for the residents of the towers. Large terraces create connections between the commercial and residential towers.

01: One Island East is a flexible urban plaza for a commercial office tower that incorporates the intimate scale of a residential urban landscape. **02:** A formal language of subtly shifting rhomboids gives structure to the site and negotiates a significant grade change from one end of the terraces to the far end of the plaza. **03:** At the entrance of the new office tower the fountain is programmed to create different water and lighting effects.

A formal language of subtly shifting rhomboids provides structure for the site and negotiates a significant grade change from one end of the terraces to the far end of the plaza. The irregular form of the rhomboids shape the overall form and the subtleties of the site, adeptly transitioning the grades through the stepped structures. As the grade moves irregularly through the plaza, sloping away on one side and remaining constant on the other, the rhomboid unifies the spatial experience of the site. At each of the rhomboid forms, cascade fountains pool water at the top of the plaza and send the flowing water over a series of illuminated granite knife edges into basins at the base of the forms. Step terraces border the cascades and create seating, which complements a wide range of built-in seating across the site. The lower part of the plaza provides the garden like setting with lush tropical vegetation and water elements, creating a passive recreation space for the residents at the plaza.

The design incorporates complex details within the plaza, including curving hardwood benches that are illuminated with internal LED lights, and a cantilevered granite bench that peels off from the groundplane. The design also incorporates a series of fountains that integrate the landform structures and plaza with the movement of water. At the entrance of the new office tower, Hargreaves designed an artesian interactive fountain that can be programmed to create different water and lighting effects. Another fountain takes the form of an egg with large, black granite bars spaced apart. Between the bars, white water spray completes the overall form. This entry area of the new commercial tower can be used for exhibitions of all kinds for the towers. Hargreaves Associates successfully designed a plaza space in Hong Kong that is flexible, allowing the needs of a commercial tower with the more intimate scale of a residential urban landscape.

01: At each of the rhomboids, cascade fountains pool water at the top of the plaza and send the flowing water over a series of illuminated granite knife edges into basins at the base. **02:** The design incorporates complex details within the plaza. **03:** The lower part of the plaza provides the garden like setting with lush tropical vegetation and water elements.

01

02

03

These discrete landscapes present rarified, cogent ideas at the scale of the garden and small urban plaza. With specific programs and a finer grain of detail, these smaller projects are not laboratories for larger projects, but a distinct part of the firm's practice. Programs on these sites are less far-reaching than large parks, but are still complex, and typically require several types of spaces within the design. Plazas of display are integrated with more passive, contemplative areas for shaded sitting while vibrant fountains coexist with horticultural gardens. In each of the projects the local conditions inform the overall narrative of the design as well as the materiality of the landscape features and plantings. Custom details of fountains and benches further define the identity of these places, creating strong designs with distinct design language. Smaller projects offer immersive landscape experiences with finely tuned choreographies of movement and perception.

01.02: Custom designed curving hardwood benches are illuminated with internal LED lights. **03:** The interactive fountain by the office tower entrance. **04:** The site accommodates a range of daytime uses. **05:** Black granite and white water spray complete the form of the egg-shaped fountain. **06:** The design shapes intimate spaces for the residents.

04   05   06

01

02

03

04

01.02: The rhomboid forms give shape and negotiate differences in grade and program across the site. 03.04: Step terraces border the cascades and create seating, which complements a wide range of built-in seating across the site.

AGENCY BY DESIGN

JULIA CZERNIAK

Urban parks have agency. Yet for most people, the landscape type "park" still conjures up images of publically amended green spaces for relaxation and recreation. For landscape architects and others versed in the rich variety of North America's nineteenth- and twentieth-century parks – from large working systems such as Boston's Emerald Necklace to representations of nature in pocket sites such as Paley Park in New York – how parks look, what they do, and how they are organized and used has expanded considerably, in large part through disciplinary interest and provocative design thinking that embrace how landscapes unfold in time as social, political, and ecological processes.

What is less understood to both the public and practitioners is the way in which well-designed urban parks are catalysts – agents that accelerate change or recovery – to the development and redevelopment of cities. When Frederick Law Olmsted and Calvert Vaux designed Central Park, they understood the relationship between building parks and building cities. Although the core of New York's population was still 2.5 miles from the park in 1858, Olmsted and Vaux anticipated the recreational needs of residents of nineteenth-century North American industrial cities. They recognized that land acquired for a large park – in this case, where the park came before the city – would easily pay for itself over time with increasing land values at its perimeter. Today designers, developers, and politicians find themselves dealing with different sites. Rather than greenfields on the outskirts of emerging and thriving cities, they face brownfields in often shrinking urban downtowns characterized by decaying and abandoned buildings, crumbling infrastructure, toxicity, disinvestment, fragmented use, and loss of tax base and population.

Hargreaves Associates have built a practice known for its advanced design, technical expertise, public engagement, and the ability to get projects built in a context of complex politics and tough economics. Their work is admired for its ability to make something from nothing – extraordinary landscapes created from the dross of the city. This essay examines parks located in distressed post-industrial environments that are coming back to life. These projects, all built except for the London 2012 Olympic Park, currently being envisioned, suggest that through

a combination of thoughtful and rigorous design strategies, parks are agents for urban revitalization. Agency here suggests a shift in landscape's passive role as picture or ground.[1] The park as green oasis is supplemented by parks whose design strategies set in motion, even accelerate, positive change in the decaying cities in which they are located. Hargreaves Associates have advanced strategies that, across scale, foreground connectivity, impassioned use, strong identity, and design innovation. In so doing, these parks transform not only their physical environments but also the economic and social realities of the city.

Connectivity

When urban planner Kevin Lynch described "paths" for the traditional city of districts, nodes, and landmarks, he portrayed streets, walks, transit lines, canals, and roads as elements along which people move and observe the city.[2] For Hargreaves Associates, connectors within the contemporary city of ambiguous space, fragmented use, and disjunction are more than movement corridors – they create physical, visual, and site-specific relationships at nested scales between the body and the city and act as important supports for collective life. For parks to catalyze distressed sites, large physical connections of urban infrastructure – highways, roads, pathways, rail lines, or waterways – must knit the landscape into the fabric of the city. Well-designed circulation for walking or biking that connect a park's amenities are also essential. New visual corridors within parks enable a reconnection between cities and neglected assets such as rivers. More abstractly, connections to a site's specific conditions – whether a significant event or a material, experiential, or phenomenal attribute – ground the design in a place. Finally, as contemporary park sites are often fragmented from the natural resources they need, connections must be made to facilitate flows of water, nutrients, and energy that are essential for maintaining the ecological health of parks. In all of these ways, connections are less simple links than they are initiators of complex and nuanced relationships.

The connective possibilities of Discovery Green in Houston are linked to its organizational strategy. Like most parks – including the adjacent Root Memorial Square Park, whose organization

Fig 1

Fig 2

Fig 3

Fig 4

is characterized by sinuous curves – its palette is constituted by grass, trees, water, pathways, plazas, buildings, play areas, and other programs. But unlike them, this new 12-acre urban park is organized largely by parallel bands of different widths running roughly east/west in the direction of downtown, which emphasize views of the skyline. Although this organization in not necessarily new to parks (we have seen these programmatic bands used in OMA's 1994 competition scheme for La Villette in Paris, drawing on a tradition that goes back to the Romans), the use of a wide pedestrian path that punctuates this arrangement provides an important and highly programmed link between two sports complexes at each edge of the site. Unlike the bands at La Villette, these bands enable a strong relationship between the park's organizational diagram and its extension into its context, creating a seamless connection between the park and the city, while through its juxtaposition of use, providing a needed break from it. Additionally, activities at the park edges extend adjacent building uses, knitting the park into its context: the bars and restaurants of a hotel lobby release people into colorful urban gardens, while the convention center opens onto a large urban green framed with donor walls, an amphitheater, and access to underground parking.

In Baton Rouge, the strategy of connectivity is activated in the Shaw Center for the Arts by two nested scales of spatial sequence that link downtown to the Mississippi River, currently obstructed by a levee and severed from the city by degraded parking lots and decaying property. The Center and its attendant program, located on just one city block (known as the Arts Block), is anchored by the building program of performing arts theater and museum, and the landscape program of plaza, street, and existing park – a small, historic but withering place distinguished by an antique water tower, Live Oak trees, and views of the river. At the scale of the block, a field of differently sized, shaped, and colored pavers organized in alternating bands is a new continuous ground plane that is both extensive in its continuity and diversified in its use (fig. 1). This treatment incorporates the space of and reinforces a pedestrian sequence from the downtown, along an entrance alley, through the museum lobby, and across the plaza, street, and adjacent park to a view of the Mississippi.

This sequence is amplified by a series of thresholds – from outside to inside spaces, from warm to cool temperatures, through lines of water, pedestrians, and cars, to alternating hard and soft environments produced by remarkable tree canopies and lush ground plantings.

Hargreaves Associates' early masterplan work for the Baton Rouge waterfront suggests strategies for connecting city to water at a different scale. Here the Arts Block was conceptualized as part of Baton Rouge's "front lawn," a term the designers used to refer to a large constellation of civic spaces, including a government plaza, state capitol, and town square, as well as open space adjacent to the river. Whereas the sequence through the Shaw Center unfolds along a ground plane and provides views of the Mississippi, the projected sequence at the city scale is based on a complex section that would allow people river access through new pedestrian bridges and crossings, riverfront terraces at different levels, and decks.

A severed connection to waterfronts is something many cities share, and Hargreaves Associates are known for their expertise in revitalizing this link. As Louisville, Kentucky, grew, it developed a bustling relationship to the Ohio River, but gradually lost this tie over time as modes of transport – railroad lines, service roads, and highways – limited public access to the river's edge. At the scale of urban infrastructure, strategies for reconnecting downtown Louisville to its waterfront included rerouting traffic, moving on-ramps, reconfiguring the water's edge, and designing a continuous pedestrian and bicycle system that knits park and city and ensures convenient access to all program components. More powerfully, however, is the effect of sloping the ground plane of the park's major public event space, the Great Lawn, whose presence is exacerbated by its shift off the grid geometry of the rest of the city. Using a strategy similar to one deployed at the wharf, where a paved plane gently slopes into and disappears under the water's edge, the designers lowered the grade below the elevated highway that passes through the site, accentuating views to and across the river and making the space underneath less of a physical barrier. By associating the barrier produced by the highway with its negative psychological effects and addressing

Fig 5

Fig 6

Fig 7

them through lighting strategies, strips of green lawn, and a series of powerful urban frames, the designers successfully transformed this previously unpleasant space into a new kind of urban place.

The 21st Century Waterfront Park relies on similar tactics of physical and visual connection to unite downtown Chattanooga to the Tennessee River, connections that amplify the river's complex flood regimens and steep edges. Inhabitable spaces along, over, and within the river join forces with a new marina to lead people out onto the water, on floating platforms that change positions with water level and commercial and private boats accessed by flexible ramps. Both modes reconnect individuals with water in visceral ways through shifting grounds and fluid movements. The park's steep site sponsors a remarkable section that unfolds as a complex spatial experience accented by design elements that navigate steep inclines. Beginning on a floating walk along the Tennessee, one moves up through a Piranesian network of bridges, stairs, and ramps that undergirds a highway and leads, higher still, to a pedestrian bridge that brings you back over the river where you began.[3] (fig. 2) The path's final ascent to the bluff is integrated into an existing series of ramped switchbacks similar in form to Lombard Street in San Francisco. The development of this seemingly innocuous sequence of connective infrastructure (a ramp) into an imageable civic and landscape space (a sloping garden) illustrates the practice's continued ability to challenge conventions.

In Chattanooga, Hargreaves Associates deploy two additional modes of connection evident in many of their projects – advancing design features that link to the history of the site and proposing ecological networks that unite living systems. One example of the first is seven ceramic medallions created by Cherokee artists for the underground passage between the aquarium and Ross's Landing in the 21st Century Waterfront Park. Here, public art honors the Cherokees who were part of the "Trail of Tears," the route used in forced relocation of Native Americans, passing through the site. Unique features such as these that come from the history of the site (are connected in *that way*) help to constitute these parks' identities. Finally, the habitat for native plants and animals in Renaissance Park's constructed wetland

on the north side of the Tennessee River is sustained only through careful attention to water flows. The emergent plantings of cattail, bulrush, and rose mallow require that water captured from a nearby urban stream and storm-water collected on site be maintained through the interconnection of constructed civil systems.

Use

For an urban park to accelerate change to its local context, it must enrich culture and the lives of those who use it. Most parks contain an extensive range of program and activities that support the city. In some, program is viewed as the instrument that drives organization and form, from the requirements of playing fields to those of parking lots.[4] The programming of parks is dynamic, responding to the needs and desires of users, and parks must be resilient enough to accommodate these changes without ongoing restructuring.[5] How people use parks thus depends on many things – their given program, their material surfaces, and even the weather. Yet unscripted, nonprogrammed use may be what attracts people to the same park again and again. Like many design practices, Hargreaves Associates have been subject to increasing pressure to program their parks with a seemingly endless list of activities. What makes these urban parks different, however, is their careful attention to not just accommodating the right balance of events and activities specific to a place and the needs of its users, but creating smart and sensuous stages where urban life plays out. These stages are enabled by their design strategies which advance multifunctioning elements at different scales and by the varied use of materials and surfaces.

When Robert Venturi wrote of "double-functioning elements" in architecture, he cited examples of ambiguous correspondences between form and function both generally (such as where structure plays a spatial role) and specifically in details (such as where windows become niches).[6] In landscape, the conflation of *infra*structure projects with civic spaces is common. Hargreaves Associates themselves are known for projects where infrastructural demands are aligned with recreation: landfill/park (Candlestick Point Cultural Park, 1985); flood control/park (Guadalupe River Park, 1988; Louisville Waterfront Park, 1999); waste disposal/park (Byxbee Park, 1988); water treatment/

festival area (Sydney Olympics, 1999); roadway infrastructure/parkway (Fort Washington Way, 2002); constructed wetland/park (Renaissance Park, 2006). Addressing the formal, social, and engineering concerns of each site yield landscape elements that unconventionally double perform, such as landfill rubble that becomes site furnishing or landform that directs flows of water and people.

More recent parks offer a different scale of form/function conflation. The north/south "promenade" that cuts through the programmatic bands at Discovery Green – a high-intensity urban surface with activities that attract both contemporary urbanites and local families – no longer simply plays its historic role as an axial tree-lined route for people to walk along and be seen. Here it becomes an asymmetric programmatic spine replete with demountable pavilions for markets and crafts events, as well as peripheral uses such as upscale restaurants, interactive fountains, and model boat basins. This promenade contrasts the more conventional walkway shaded by 100-year-old Live Oaks that runs perpendicular to it.

Yet it is one strategy to design park spaces and elements with double functions; it is another to project indeterminacy so that users can make decisions for themselves. As Alex Wall has suggested and these parks show, "a design that can accommodate many functions is both economical and enriching of social space…making things and places that are indeterminate in their functions…allow their users to invent and claim space for themselves. Such investment by the users subsequently ensures a long and affectionate occupation of public space."[7] Something as simple as moveable furniture, an element seen frequently in urban parks, provides users with the power to participate in the making of space. A mother's ability to move a chair in order to watch over her playing children, for instance, provides a sense of control. A more significant example is systemic moments that emerge from the design logic itself, such as those in Louisville Waterfront Park. Many of the remarkable places within this park, such as the Great Lawn's large, gently sloping gathering space, or small picnic areas nestled between landforms and shaded tree groves, are distributed across the park at different levels. The transitions between them – through stairs, ramps, and walls – produce new kinds of spaces and activities. Hargreaves Associates President Mary Margaret Jones describes the strategy used to produce them as "gathering grade," or imbuing the basic need to transition between heights with the energy of a social space.[8] (fig. 3) In this instance, a simple stair along the Great Lawn becomes theater, stage, platform, and podium.

Attracting people to parks requires more, however, than a variety of programs, however planned or unplanned. When Olmsted was designing Central Park, for instance, he argued for well-drained footpaths so that women, on exiting their carriages, could protect their dresses from moisture and soil. In other words, parks have to be comfortable places that meet a remarkable diversity of needs. Hargreaves Associates develop the material palettes for the ground planes and three-dimensional places of their parks to express programmatic use, provoke new activity, and produce sensory effects. The diverse materials that articulate the horizontal plane of Houston's Discovery Green – grass, concrete, wood, recycled rubber, crushed stone, even granite – animate the ground with color, texture, and scale all the while performing as thermal reflectors, absorptive sponges, and durable surfaces. (fig. 4) These characteristics matter to people who use them in different seasons, times of day, and for various occasions. Plant materials and lighting fixtures are just two examples of elements that articulate and define a park's spaces and produce varied effects. Nothing compares to the palpable relief you feel as you move from the sweltering sunlight on Jones Lawn on a 104-degree June day into the cool and fragrant shade of the Oak allée. The rising glow of accent lights as day transitions to evening and the colorful massings and intricate textures of plant material in the tropical and regional gardens provide other sensory experiences.

Identity

Parks as agents in urban revitalization require strong identities to make them distinct from their contexts and generate use, publicity, and revenue. When designing parks, Hargreaves Associates are less concerned with their park's image (the immediacy of its look) than with its identity (its distinguishing character that accrues over time), evident through form (organization, shape, and size), relationship to site (physically and referentially), and relationship between the temporal and the

permanent. A park's identity is also formed by the way it comes to be regarded by its users – from well-manicured, maintained, and secure (as at Discovery Green) to open and allowed to evolve dramatically over time (as at Candlestick Point or Byxbee Parks). Despite what appears to be the firm's repeated design lexicon of strong geometries and sculptural landforms, each of their parks is a unique place made by specific design strategies and features deployed at multiple scales. In this way, Hargreaves Associates' interest in identity refers to the condition of each park's being singular – one park and not another in place and time.

The contemporary identity of the Shaw Center for the Arts is established by the alternating bands of the ground plane that sit in stark contrast to the adjacent historical landscape of Repentance Park, the Old State Capitol and grounds, and the traditional architecture of the auto hotel (a former 1930s parking garage), which it spans. The block's fresh character is accentuated by the building's glass and aluminum skin, whose organization mirrors the banding of the ground, strengthening its impact. The building and site design together reinforce the ambition to consolidate public open space and coordinate public/private investment and development. The project succeeds by leveraging an arts program and a distinctive landscape design that combine the typologies of building interior, plaza, street, and park into a recognizable whole.

At Louisville, what the designers refer to as "pulling the open space of the river into the city"[9] – and not simply extending the city grid to it – sets up the framework for the park's powerful identity based on how a landscape both appears and performs.[10] By appearance I mean how parks look, the impressions they give, and their processes of coming into being. Performance suggests how parks work and what they accomplish. The interlocking of land and water at different scales through "inlets," which appear as an abstraction of a local stream network that drains into metropolitan Louisville, provides a stage for visitors to interact with river processes. The primary one, called the Harbor Inlet, allows watercraft to dock and thereby signals the return of once thriving river-related activity to the downtown core. More interesting, however, is the smaller inlet to the east. Nine years after the park's completion, this inlet has become a wetland and a favorite

place for birding, an evolution dependent on the flows of the Ohio River, silt infill, and emergent plant communities. (fig. 5) It also suggests strategies for park design where landscape is both representational (it refers to river forms and past activities) and performative (it actually changes by engaging river processes). In this way, Louisville Waterfront Park is a powerful example of a park's identity being constituted by stable and meaningful references that are also responsive to the fluxes of the landscape medium.

The play between a design lexicon and its deployment on a specific site characterizes all of Hargreaves Associates' parks and is commonly driven by the physical aspects of a place, such as existing geometries, and by latent characteristics, such as a site's history. Some projects, like Byxbee Park in Palo Alto, abound with modest and subtle references to their locations.[11] More common to their practice, a site drives both large and small design moves. For instance, Chattanooga's natural features and the site's adjacent development characteristics guide the organization of the Waterfront Park into six distinct districts. One of these districts is marked by a sculptural fountain that recalls the jumping off point for the Trail of Tears, mentioned earlier. Both organizational strategies set the framework for smaller design decisions, such as the addition of site-specific art. In all of these examples, a park's identity is constituted by the designer's play with particular references to a place.

Perhaps most interesting is a designer's attitude toward how parks' either "age" or "change" – two views of time with vastly different implications – which affects their identity. An aging park is different than an emergent one: picture failing pavement, broken light fixtures, and weathered furnishings over the slow and beautiful transition from field to forest. Hargreaves Associates embrace both ends of the spectrum, with strategies that both "speed-up or slow-down the process of nature."[12] Discovery Green, paid for mostly by private dollars, has a not-for-profit conservancy that maintains it to very high standards. Not to be underestimated in the perception of the park are the efforts of those who clean and repair it each day, maintenance and operations appropriate to a heavily used urban park attempting to revive a downtown core. At the other end of the spectrum is Candlestick Point Cultural Park, built on landfill extending into the San Francisco Bay, and used less frequently by outdoor enthusiasts and tourists. Candlestick Point is an exquisite spectacle of decay-by-design. The edges of the inclined plane, once crisp, are now less definite, eroded as they are by the forces of the site. (fig. 6) Successional shrubs have infiltrated both it and the surrounding once-sculpted landforms. Embracing entropy in this way, the designers allowed the inevitable deterioration of a system to characterize this park. Louisville Waterfront Park shares aspects of both strategies – some areas evolve through water-borne seeding while others are highly manicured.

Innovation

What give urban parks the most agency – that is, their power to activate change – is innovative design that challenges convention, proposes invention, and embraces experimentation. Without these qualities, new parks would neither hold the imagination nor attract the resources of people who pay for and use them long enough to work through the complex political and economic processes necessary to realize them. Hargreaves Associates have, since their formation, challenged the premise that design is problem solving driven by function. They have rallied against the conventional and kept to an early premise by George Hargreaves: "As landscape architects, we need to get off the functional diagram and develop meanings in our projects. We can tuck in the more functional aspects as opposed to making them what it's all about."[13]

Although the problems design professionals face have changed over the last half century, even a casual acquaintance with the discipline recognizes the growing call for sustainable landscapes. In the broadest sense, sustainability is the capacity to support certain processes, be they economic or ecologic. In its ecological sense, sustainability is the ability of an ecosystem to maintain functions, biodiversity, and productivity into the future.[14] Although Hargreaves Associates has led the field in advancing process-based landscapes that foreground ecologic, social, and economic performance, "green" and "sustainable" are two words not often used by this firm to legitimate its work. This is in part due to the now commonplace use of brownfield remediation strategies, storm-water treatment, and the preference for native plants

as the responsible way to build. Although green and sustainable principles are present in Hargreaves Associates' work, they are never the raison d'etre of the project but simply part of the design equation – similar in value to the use of landform as space-maker or to the formal attributes of trees. In this way the firm innovates relationships among how parks look, what they mean, and the feelings they prompt with the sound, sustainable services they provide in inventive and surprising ways.

Most users of Discovery Green are probably unaware that the park is constructed of local building materials and native plants. They most likely will not notice the large banks of photovoltaic panels and solar water-heating elements integrated into the veranda shade structures that significantly offset the park's energy consumption.[15] (fig. 6) And the mechanics of water collection that refill the park's lake in lieu of discharging storm-water into the city's system are not even visible. Yet visitors may feel the cool breezes channeled across the site from strategically placed architectural and landscape elements; they may notice the quality of natural northern light enabled by the wide expanses of glazing; and they may appreciate the shade cast by the southern verandas as relief from the hot Texas sun. What users will remember from their time at Discovery Green is a vibrant and wildly successful place that has catalyzed a small part of their city.

Its location in a flood zone drives a set of design strategies for the Louisville Waterfront. A majority of the park is designed to withstand temporary flooding through such techniques as slope stabilization, the use of fast-draining soils and strengthened lawns, and durable furnishings.[16] These conventional approaches are not surprising. What is surprising is the conception of the Great Lawn as a surface that enables floodwater and debris to quickly recede, or the way that program is placed according to its ability to withstand the strong forces of water. Through many visits to the park I have appreciated the Great Lawn for the visual and physical access it provides to the Ohio, not its drainage properties, however important in cities such as Louisville that have a history of combined sewer overflows.[17] This detail demonstrates that what may be overlooked by users is a priority to clients, and to those whose state and federal funding sources are tied to this level of performance.

Prioritizing cleaning and managing water through green infrastructure elements such as roof gardens, bio-swales, rain-gardens, and porous surfaces has for many cities led to the economic growth of their waterfronts.[18] Green infrastructural strategies are one aspect of sustainable practice in common – though often uninspired – use by many landscape architects. Hargreaves Associates' small constructed wetland in Chattanooga's Renaissance Park is designed to treat the first flush of urban runoff from a surrounding catchment zone before it enters the Tennessee River. Not only does it harness the latest technologies, it does so through forms and toward effects that are both beautiful and surprising. Most generally, this area of the park joins other Hargreaves projects by encapsulating contaminated soils on site in extreme landforms that create an intricacy of spaces textured by native grasses, lawns, and paving. Overlaid onto this new topography are traditional park elements and activities: seating, lighting, picnic benches, paths for strolling and biking, and bridges from which to watch birds. Unlike an Olmsted park that focuses on a bucolic scene, this hybridization of green infrastructure with urban park that foregrounds the cleaning process of impure water is powerfully different. It is precisely this wetland's arrangement that announces its innovation. (fig. 8) The compact site precludes the use of more conventional wetland meanders essential to the filtration process. The addition of strategically organized gabions asks the water to follow a longer path, directing its flow around the plant cells, wire mesh structures filled with emergent aquatic vegetation that filter pollutants by the biological action of microbes.[19]

Projecting Futures: London 2012

If it is possible to take a cue from the success of Discovery Green, the Shaw Center for the Arts, the Louisville Waterfront, and Chattanooga's 21st Century Park as agents in urban regeneration, then the future of the site of the London Olympics – the most comprehensive and high-profile project with which Hargreaves Associates are currently involved – looks quite optimistic. The site for Discovery Green was characterized by blocks of surface parking, electrical power infrastructure, and remnant fabric on vacant sites – uses incompatible with a thriving urban core. Through design strategies that strongly link park and city, create a legible destination, and provide much-needed activity and landscape program, Discovery Green has already proven to be an extremely effective catalyst for the adjacent redevelopment of office towers and hotels. The success of the Shaw Center as an agent for the city bore out the beliefs of the original stakeholders: that a project grounded in the visual and performing arts, and strategically designed, has the potential to stimulate the growth of their city. Since that time, its use and identity has sponsored the development of market-rate housing at the Arts Block perimeter. Even before the designers were selected for Louisville, the Waterfront Development Corporation foresaw the remaking of the Ohio's blighted edge into a vibrant park and catalyst for business and waterfront redevelopment.[20] By all accounts, the designers met the developer's expectations: the park has paved the way for other important projects such as Slugger Field and Waterfront Park Place, and has indirectly influenced residential and commercial growth in the area.[21] The story in Chattanooga is similar. Through strategies that connect the Tennessee River to the city in both obvious and complex ways – providing a broad range of program and activities, producing a strong identity, and pushing the limits of the landscape discipline – the design contributed to restoring downtown's vitality through the dual notions of public access and quality development.[22]

Sited on formerly contaminated industrial land in a river valley to the northeast of the city known as the "East End," one of the most heavily bombed sites in London, the 2012 Olympic Park advances the strategies of agency used by Hargreaves in their earlier urban parks.[23] In addition to the vast network of physical connectors – roads, bridges, paths, bus lanes, and other modes of public transportation infrastructure – that must accommodate 250,000 spectators daily, the park design is based on the restoration of the previously neglected and channelized River Lea, around which settlements and villages thrived in both pre-industrial and industrial times. The promise of the park's identity lies in its rich tapestry of reference to both the river and its processes and the centuries of park design and gardening embedded in British culture.

The Olympic Park's division into northern and southern sections – the north focused on water management and habitat creation, and the south on programs for the festival itself such as gardens, markets, and cafes – gave the designers the opportunity to extend the green infrastructure strategies used by them at the Green Games in Sydney. Although the site's soils are now heavily polluted, after soil washing the designers are strategically shaping the ground, forming its slopes and placing its landform objects in ways that enable visual connections to and contact with the river. This new topography is in no small part the result of a mandate not to export any soil, requiring the reuse of up to 300,000 cubic yards of fill. The focus on habitat creation and the desire to treat water biologically prompted the use of more woodlands and wetlands, frog ponds, meadows, reedbeds, and grassy swales, producing more than 700 artificial habitats for hundreds of common and rare species. More important, unlike in many environments geared toward the development of biodiversity, the designers developed strategies that integrate human activity with habitat formation – no fences or other barriers keep park users out. In this way, the northern end of the Olympic Park will be one of the most progressive, albeit experimental, examples of conflating seemingly opposing uses. (fig. 8) The southern end, characterized by a one-half-mile long sequence of gardens, traces the history of British plant acquisition through the centuries and from around the world. Organized by hemisphere, each garden uses plant in ways that facilitate adaptation to the local climate and produces a contemporary expression that promises to be an international attraction for the Games, and after for regional visitors.[24] (fig. 9)

Although it is difficult to predict precisely how visitors will use the site during the festivities, designing for what is called "games mode" and "transformation mode" is central to the work. A key aspect of the project's planning process has been the development of a spatial plan for the Olympic Park site after the 2012 games, referred to by its organizers as the Legacy Masterplan. The organizers are already considering the system of footpaths, cycleways, and avenues of trees that will link the park with existing and future communities during and after the event. This plan will also play an important role in ensuring the continued services of flood protection and water management that the park is planning to provide and that remain crucial to the sustained viability of local habitat. As Hargreaves points out,

"these parks will be considered a success by not only how they celebrate the games but also how they extend a green Olympic Legacy into the future."[25]

It is hard to imagine cities without thriving parks, ones that provide relief from urban intensity and ones that provoke it; parks that are characterized by expanses of beautiful scenery, pastoral prospects, and diversity of wildlife and ones with a density of programs and activities provided or suggested by users. Yet to conceive of landscape solely in this role is to suspend its instigative potential, its ability to activate and accelerate change to the environments in which it participates. These parks by Hargreaves Associates reflect this enhanced scope of engagement, helping to give the urban contexts in which they are located another chance.

Fig 8

Fig 9

URBAN PARKS

01

DISCOVERY GREEN
Houston, Texas

Hargreaves Associates' design of urban parks is responsive to the unique requirements of the urban environment, reflecting the perceptions, needs and desires of their communities. The 19th century model of park as retreat to nature still holds currency in the public eye as the prevailing view of the public urban park, regardless of a dramatic shift in the performance and integration of urban parks in every aspect of city life. Urban parks provide amenities for their immediate neighborhoods, and, depending on the scale of the park, for the city and region as a whole. Depending on the context, urban parks can emphasize highly programmed activities, flexible play spaces, quiet areas for contemplation, the relationship to nature in the built environment, and frequently all of these at once. In order to facilitate the effectiveness of parks, Hargreaves Associates develops organized strategies for program and incorporates public process. The firm's design of urban parks focuses on an exploration of a concise body of clear ideas, creating a comprehensive attitude toward history, ecology, landscape form and program. These urban parks maximize positive impacts for their communities, manifesting local expressions of site while activating the parks through strategic regimes of program organization.

Ecological functioning is a key concern for Hargreaves Associates' urban parks, which can recreate native ecologies, contributing both to habitat and reinforcing the locality of a place. In other cases the design employs performative landscape structures that remediate a brownfield site or contribute to citywide stormwater efforts through rain gardens or larger scale constructed wetlands. These parks have vital ecological and social roles. At the same time, a series of successful public/private partnerships, pairing parks with business improvement districts and other creative alliances have provided valuable precedent for cities. Cities are growing more and more savvy in the creation and maintenance of parks, investigating all models of public/private partnerships and redefining the way public space is made possible. Hargreaves Associates has worked on many parks that rely on public/private partnerships. These projects demonstrate a keen understanding of the political realities of the day, and show how landscape architects can play a role in the long range economic planning of the city. Julia Czerniak, in her essay in this book, discusses how specific design elements in Hargreaves Associates' public parks create agency for larger movements of urban revitalization.

02

01: Discovery Green has a dense and varied program, drawing diverse users to the city center. **02**: The park also reflects Houston's strong garden heritage.

01

Discovery Green, completed in 2008 with the intention of helping to revitalize Houston's challenged downtown, is a park with dense and varied program, drawing diverse users to the city center. The park is the signature open space of downtown Houston, the first effort in a project to catalyze the transformation of the urban core of the city from a landscape of surface parking lots and unprogrammed open space into a vital, street-life oriented environment. Located beside the George R. Brown Convention Center, the Hilton Americas Hotel, and nearby two major arena venues – Minute Maid Park, home of the Houston Astros, and Toyota Center, a sporting and performance venue – the twelve-acre park accommodates the intermittent usage of these event-oriented spaces, while providing a neighborhood anchor to foster residential and commercial developments.

A strategic alliance of civic leaders and private individuals, corporate and institutional interests came together in order to build the park, with the long-term goal of activating downtown as a whole. The project was initiated by a public/private partnership between the Houston Downtown Park Corporation, the city government, and the Discovery Green Conservancy, a private non-profit that has taken on the long-term stewardship of the park. The City of Houston donated land and funds to add to the initial parcel, and contributed to the construction budget of the below grade parking structure directly under the park. The Discovery Green Conservancy raised funds to construct the park and continues to maintain the park's activities, raising funds through philanthropy, sponsorships, events, and through the rents and proceeds of the on-site restaurants. The City of Houston also contributes one third of the annual maintenance costs of the park.

At Discovery Green, Hargreaves Associates designed a park whose structure would support the development goals of the client group, beginning with ensuring a well-populated active park. With an absence of street life, a landscape of surface parking lots and vacant lots dominating the district, the client group was initially skeptical that the park would find a constituency. A fundamental goal of the design process was to create a park that people would visit and make many return visits. At the same time, the client desired a soft, green respite from the Houston heat, a place that would reflect Houston's strong garden heritage.

01-03: Within the Urban Garden are horticultural garden collections, sculpture, and clearings for active recreation such as bocce and shuffleboard. **04**: Bands of program lock into The Crawford Promenade, an activated spine of activity.

01

01.02: The interactive fountain is a magnet for young children in the Houston heat.

01

01-03: The design crafts a distinct urban identity through the programmatic bands of the park.

Hargreaves Associates developed a systematic treatment of dense program, activating the site for different user groups and all times during the day, while at the same time creating large areas of open lawn and shady areas of trees. The park design maximizes diversity and density of program through a system of layered program over the underlying circulation structure of the park. The program that became incorporated into the park was developed through a series of public workshops with the community before and during the design process.

Existing lines on the site – a through street, and perpendicular to it, a healthy Live Oak Allée – provided a structure to form Discovery Green's axial circulation system. The City closed the through street, incorporating it into the park. In the Hargreaves Associates design this forms the Crawford Promenade,

02

03

a generous pedestrian north/south walkway. The Promenade is an activated spine of activity, with bands of program locking into this circulation axis. This arrangement concentrates active programming that requires paving along one linear strip and allows for consolidated open green space in the other areas of the park. Additionally, the concentration of movement along the Crawford Promenade ensures that the park feels active even with a low volume of users. In counterpoint, the historic Live Oak Allée, over one hundred years old, creates the other axis of the site, a shady respite in the park with a limestone pathway, small seating areas and bollards that cast light into the canopy of the trees.

Linear strips of program lock into the Crawford Promenade, forming rough zones of open space types. The open space types organize gardens (the Urban Gardens, Market Grove, and Event Lawn) across one zone, lawns (the Great Lawn and a picnic lawn) across another, and water (wetland pond, model boat pond and interactive fountains) across another. Additional strips of structures (Café, Restaurant, and Park Offices) also lock into the Crawford Promenade. The interaction of the program elements and the Promenade creates a cohesive experience as program reaches from one side of the Promenade to the other in continuous banding. The zones are organized so that the experience of being in each one feels dominant, and changes as the visitor moves throughout the site. This shifting feeling of center is reinforced thorough designed views out to the city from within each individual band.

Program is proliferated within each of the major programmatic zones, creating multitudes of activities and uses at different scales.

Program elements with different audiences, scales and characters are layered within the bands, structured by their relationship to the major circulation axes. This organization facilitates slippage between program elements rather than the containment of program in a structured, defined area. Within the Urban Garden there are horticultural garden collections, which prompt passive recreation, as well as clearings for active recreation such as bocce and shuffleboard. Native Texas plants as well as traditional garden plants of Texas are used to craft horticultural collections within the garden rooms. Incorporating art within the Urban Garden, the Listening Vessels sculpture amplifies ambient sounds. The Urban Garden zone also contains the Event Lawn, which accommodates smaller events like weddings and restaurant functions.

The Great Lawn is an open space that allows for a range of activities such as picnicking, pickup sports games, sunbathing, reading, a virtually limitless range of self-defined activities. Adjacent to the Great Lawn is the Amphitheater Slope, which hosts synergistic programs of larger concerts and performances. The slope of the amphitheater expresses the tectonics of the ramped roof of the parking garage below. The above ground manifestations of the parking garage – ventilation and stairwells – are designed to reinforce the park experience. The ventilation areas are clad in elegant wooded slats, and a public art work entitled *Synchronicity of Color,* a patchwork of bright powder coated steel cubes of color, is placed at the stairwell protrusions.

The *Water* elements of the site are located on the northern edge, with a passive pond with wetland edges and Model Boat Area transitioning across the Crawford Promenade into an Interactive Fountain. The family-oriented programming is focused at the western end of the site, closest to the planned residential towers. The play area at the edge of the park is a gathering space for young families and the Interactive Fountain and *Mist Tree* sculpture are magnets for young children in the Houston heat.

Hargreaves Associates located the on-site architecture – a restaurant and café – to reinforce the overall site moves, stitching together program across Crawford Promenade. The café structure runs across the promenade, and the restaurant building is also located immediately off of the promenade. The buildings follow the grain of the landscape program, integrating a significant architectural presence on the site into the overall landscape strategy. The LEED Silver certified structures use traditional building materials of Houston in contemporary forms. Hargreaves Associates' deployment of shifting, overlapping bands of program across the site is reinforced by a full-time programmer of activities for the park employed by the Discovery Green Conservancy. The site is actively programmed for diverse constituents with many special events for families, art, fitness and entertainment every day.

01

ORO editions
PO Box 150338
San Rafael, CA 94915
USA

Place Stamp Here

es

and two hotels. At Discovery Green, Hargreaves Associates explore density, diversity, and multiplicity of program in the urban park. The connection between program and landscape, seen in earlier works like the Louisville Waterfront Park, is intensified here with the densification of program.

s
ur
t
g
er,

The structure of Discovery Green, created by the intersecting linear axes, organizes active areas of program and large areas of green open space,

and also orients the park to its urban context. This underlying structure creates a strong, simple gracious design and a detailed and rich urban park experience in downtown Houston.

SOUTH WATERFRONT NEIGHBORHOOD PARK
Portland, Oregon

01: Stormwater flow and collection at the South Waterfrom Neighborhood Park. 02: The two-acre park serves the needs of a new city-planned mixed use, sustainable highrise development. 03: A loose program is nestled within the landscape typologies, emphasizing the integration of varied activities with a localized landscape experience.

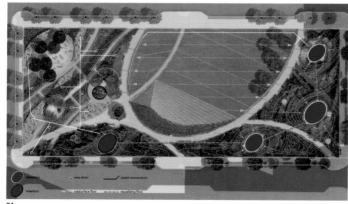

01

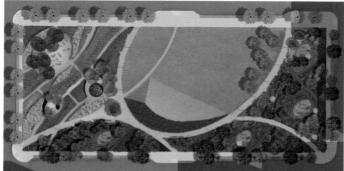

02

The **South Waterfront Neighborhood Park** also links program to landscape typology with a focus on greater ecological integration and less dense program. This park will serve a new city-planned mixed use, sustainable highrise development on a former industrial district along the Willamette River, just south of downtown Portland. The new development emphasizes sustainable practices through alternative transportation, LEED certified buildings, clean energy production and integrated stormwater management. The South Waterfront Neighborhood Park contributes to the sustainability goals of the new urban neighborhood by treating stormwater on the site and attracting wildlife. The two-acre park will serve an estimated 5000 residents and 5000 more commercial and institutional users of the immediate area. The design of the park creates an overall structure with clear spatial divisions of the site into three distinct landscape typologies. A loose program is nestled within the landscape typologies, emphasizing the integration of varied activities with a localized landscape experience.

The park is composed of a Multi-Use Lawn and two ecological landscape typologies – the Urban Garden, and the Naturalized Landscape – that emphasize the wet gardens and native forests of the Pacific Northwest. The Naturalized Landscape abstracts the lush landscape of the Pacific Northwest with a dense forest canopy punctuated by small clearings. Native plants including Western Red Cedar, Sword Fern and Oregon Grape create a woodland structure, while Columbine, Bleeding Heart, and Camass provide informal accents of seasonal color. As the entire site had been raised out of the floodplain for development purposes, the wet, undulating landscape form refigures the displaced riparian landscape of gulches and varied landforms in the park. Surface water collects across the park and infiltrates in four depressed water infiltration gardens, recharging the first flush of storm events on site and cleaning stormwater that is eventually released into the Willamette River.

03

01

02

01: The Naturalized Landscape abstracts the lush landscape of the Pacific Northwest with a dense forest canopy punctuated by small clearings. 02: The Urban Garden section of the park features a highly textured ground plane punctuated by elliptical landscape islands. 03: The added elevation of the seating slope on the Multi-use Lawn allows visitors to view the lower elevation of the Willamette River several blocks away, visually connecting the park to the waterfront.

03

The infiltration gardens are also partially irrigated by overflow water from the interactive fountain in the Urban Garden, which keeps the gardens wet and contributes to the ecological conditions of the Pacific Northwest Lowland plantings.

Clearings in the Naturalized Landscape feature an environmental artwork called *Song Cycles*, which creates soft chimes from the wind that passes through the site, making visitors aware of the environmental phenomena on site. Wood boardwalks wind through the gently undulating forest, referencing the historic waterfront.

The Naturalized Landscape and the Urban Garden have inverse spatial relationships. While the Naturalized Landscape is comprised of a dense canopy and small clearings, the Urban Garden section of the park features a highly textured groundplane punctuated by elliptical landscape islands. The landscape islands create nodes of programmed activated space, including an Environmental Play area with an interactive fountain that evokes stepping stones in a stream, a Community Gathering area with moveable tables and chairs, and a Garden Retreat for quiet contemplation. The texture

of the groundplane is created by sinuous mass plantings that can be read as a graphic from the surrounding highrise buildings. The landscape islands provide a sheltered gathering space under a tall canopy of trees within the textured groundplane. The form of the planted areas and circulation system suggests the movement of water flowing across the site, weaving through the gardens as water would carve paths over a landscape. The plantings are four-season plants, emphasizing seasonal change and reinforcing the reading of environmental phenomena on the site.

The Multi-use Lawn allows for flexible lounging space and active recreation and event space for nearby residents. The added elevation of the seating slope on the Multi-use Lawn allows visitors to view the lower elevation of the Willamette River several blocks away, visually connecting the park to the waterfront. Because of frequent rainy weather in Portland, it was important to locate the lawn in the ideal microclimate on the sunny and protected side of the site.

Though a small site, richness is layered throughout the site with largely passive yet varied program and a dedication to creating environmental

meaning on the site. The park will be the primary gathering space for the neighborhood, with retail development activating adjacent ground floor edges, while at the same time providing an ecologically rich experience of place. The landscape typologies reference native ecologies and contribute to the overall performance of this new urban district. The infiltration gardens at the South Waterfront Neighborhood Park interface with Portland's existing green stormwater infrastructure of infiltration gardens, creating a network of small scale stormwater interventions that act exponentially when taken as a whole.

01

At **South Pointe Park** in Miami Beach, Hargreaves Associates create an animated and ecologically sensitive community park in lively and flamboyant South Beach. The park is a redesign of an existing nineteen-acre park along Government Cut, an artificial inlet to Biscayne Bay at the Atlantic Ocean coast. The park positions two corresponding circulation paths – the Serpentine Walk and the Cut Walk – across its length to provide critical regional connections and views out to Government Cut and the Atlantic Ocean. The paths connect to both the Baywalk that traverses the Biscayne Bay coast, and the Beach Walk which provides access along the Atlantic Ocean. The 1800-foot long linear Cutwalk, a waterfront promenade along Government Cut, acts as a datum, rising between twelve to eighteen inches above the grade of the park across its length. The height of the path gives it the heft of a sculptural object and sets it apart from the surface of the park. Constructed from Dominican Keystone, a stone of fossilized coral, the materiality suggests the natural processes of the adjacent sea. From the park, the path is perceived both as object and line, while the experience on the path heightens the sense of spectatorship. This pathway encourages the theater of the promenade, and provides the ideal viewing platform for the massive cruise ships entering and leaving Biscayne Bay. Light pylons along the promenade were designed to co-exist with a sensitive ecological condition, the hatching of sea turtles and their migration to the ocean. During turtle nesting season, the lights illuminate the promenade with amber long wavelength light. Louvers within the pylon bounce light away from the water.

In counterpoint to the strong linear move of the Cutwalk, a serpentine landform with leisurely twists and turns begins at the Atlantic Ocean Beach Walk, rises up to allow dramatic views out to the Atlantic Ocean and access to the top of the pavilion structure, and continues west until it meets the Bay Walk. The landform encourages spirited movement along it, and as in Byxbee Park and other projects, the heightened experience of an everchanging visual field of movement is enlivened and enthralling. The twisting of the landform is echoed as a motif throughout the park in smaller garden areas. Sinuous bands of native dune plantings on the ocean side of the serpentine landform are contrasted with abstracted dune landforms and palm trees on the inside slope of the serpentine. A smaller garden area of coastal hammock plantings of native ground covers, palms and deciduous trees echo the twisting path of the landform.

01: South Pointe Park is animated and ecologically sensitive community park in lively and flamboyant Miami Beach.
02: Two corresponding circulation paths – the Serpentine Walk and the Cut Walk – provide critical regional connections and views out to Government Cut, Biscayne Bay and the Atlantic Ocean.

01

02

03

04

05

A bosque of palms with understory grasses and ferns creates a buffer to the urban context along the northern edge of the park.

The design integrates the park into the urban fabric by extending two major streets – Washington Avenue and Ocean Drive – into the park with generous hardscape entry plazas. Fountains at the Washington Avenue entrance create an urban entrance of spraying arced jets that have a sequence of water spray, which is recirculated and programmed to minimize the volume of water.

At the interior of the park, a pavilion with café and facilities creates a point of rest. A seatwall amphitheater creates an informal staging area at the pavilion, and a place for parents to watch their children at the water playground. The park also features three areas of open lawn which support free and flexible program. These areas of lawn are planted with salt tolerant turfgrasses to withstand active use and are engineered to retain water after tropical storm events. Mature trees from the site were stored during construction and then replanted on the lawn, achieving an immediate visual impact at the opening of the park.

01: The Serpentine and Cut Walks meet at sinuous dune plantings. **02,03**: The inside slope of the serpentine is contrasted with abstracted dune landforms and palm trees. **04**: The Cut Walk acts as a datum, rising between 12-18" above the grade of the park across its length. **05**: The height of the path gives it the heft of a sculptural object and sets it apart from the surface of the park.

01

01: Dune landforms restore native ecologies to the site. **02:** The park looks
to the Atlantic Ocean, with the urban street connection in the foreground.

Also within the park is a restaurant that rents the building site from the City of Miami Beach. While the restaurant activity provides revenue for the city and contributes to the ongoing maintenance of the park, incorporating the restaurant without disturbing the functioning of the park was a design challenge.

In order to bring vehicular access and parking close to the park entrance, the design creates an urban entrance edge next to the restaurant and its parking, grouping these similar elements together. The design incorporates outdoor seating terraces that flank the Cut Walk, emphasizing the circulation of the park while accommodating the restaurant programming within it.

The overall structure of South Pointe Park links it to its varied edge conditions – urban streetscape, beach promenade and cruise ship passageway. Within the park, this creates a varied and flexible structure that supports a range of activities and experiences. Through the structure of the park, Hargreaves Associates creates an ebullient landscape of spectacle and display.

ACUARIO XOCHIMILCO
Mexico City, Mexico

Hargreaves Associates is collaborating with Enrique Norten of TEN Arquitectos on **Acuario Xochimilco**, a 1300-acre historic park within the Federal District, in southern Mexico City. The large park is a complex site, providing a rage of program, infrastructure and supportive ecological systems to the region. The design team is reenvisioning the existing park, creating a healthy water, vegetation and habitat ecology for the site, rethinking the existing program and bolstering the infrastructural systems of stormwater and wastewater treatment. The redesign of Xochimilco increases access, restores appropriate ecological systems, reorganizes existing programs and sites new programs to create a park that is a local, regional, national, and international attraction.

The park has several current uses that create a rich and complex set of existing conditions. The southeastern area of the park site is comprised of *chinampas*, part of a UNESCO World Heritage Site that preserves a Pre-Columbian agricultural system still in use today. The site is located in the former lake basin of Mexico City.

Aztecs farmed in the lake basin by creating the *chinampas*, a system of man-made canals and islands of agricultural production within the lake. Though the ancient lake has dried up, the canals and the *chinampas* remain. The floating islands are still cultivated today as families tend the islands and sell fruit, vegetables and flowers at markets on the northern area of the park site.

The design for Xochimilco seeks to systematically create a robust and resilient ecology across the site. The design implements several strategies to clean the polluted site and reintroduce native ecological systems. Currently two large detention basins on site – *Ciénaga Grande* and *Ciénaga Chica* – are discharge locations for a combined stormwater and sewer overflow from the surrounding neighborhood to the west. Without proper treatment, these areas are dumping grounds, and are starting to pollute the groundwater of the area. The design for the new park separates the stormwater and sewer lines. Sewage will be redirected to a new treatment plant, and the *Ciénaga Grande* and *Ciénaga Chica* will be converted into swamp wetlands habitats that receive and clean stormwater.

02

03

01: Acuario Xochimilco is a 1300-acre historic park within the Federal District, in southern Mexico City. The large park will provide a range of program, infrastructure and supportive ecological systems to the region. **02**: A large amphitheater provides a regional concert venue. **03**: A secondary circulation system to the east connects to the *Parque ecológico*.

01

02

The swamp wetlands will feature a complete community of native plants and will support corresponding bird, aquatic and mammal species.

The entire park will be planted with native plants in specific habitat types, including wetland, forest, and meadow, as a strategy to restore ecological robustness and resilience to the site. Passive recreation meadows will be interspersed with irrigated areas of turf that can withstand intense active recreation. Freshwater lakes, ponds and streams on the site will provide habitat for the endangered Axolotl Salamander. Restoring upland forests on the site supports another dimension of a complex matrix of ecosystem types. Habitat islands in the north of the park create intense nodes to foster the success of a wide range of plant and animals. The design for Xochimilco creates a robust ecology that is necessary to shape an ongoing and evolving structure for the park.

The program works in tandem with the ecological structure. A central spine formed adjacent to the location of the existing 1968 Olympic Rowing Center organizes the site through access, circulation and program. An arrival plaza at the center of the spine, south of the periférico (highway), creates a central access point, funneling traffic from the highway and metro stop to the new aquarium, designed by TEN Arquitectos. Additional program elements are organized along the central spine. The existing flower markets are relocated along the spine, improving access for the farmers working and harvesting the chinampas, as well as for tourists that visit the site. Botanical chinampas consisting of horticultural species will provide a counterpoint to the agricultural program.New aquatic programs are sited along the spine including a new public Aquatic Center with Olympic-size pool, dive tank and beach. The pristine water for the aquarium is re-circulated through to the Aquatic Center, providing a local public amenity as well as a national tourist site. Floating botanical gardens in the form of modern chinampas extend to the north of the periférico along the central spine.

A secondary circulation system to the east connects to the Parque Ecológico, enhanced with a series of botanical garden rooms and immersive environments that explore the ecological zones of Mexico. Islands in the new swamp wetlands create additional areas for habitat and trails. A large amphitheater provides a regional concert venue. Sports fields are located along the northeast edge of the park to provide easy access to the local adjacent neighborhoods.

Xochimilco differs from other Hargreaves Associates urban parks in part because of its extremely large scale. Careful integration of ecological systems and program allows the site to be a flexible amenity, enriching the site at many scales. As a UNESCO site, the park will draw international tourists. The new Aquatic Center and Botanical Gardens will be a national resource for the country to celebrate Mexican ecologies. The new amphitheater will be a regional venue for entertainment – concerts and theater. Locally, the park will provide infrastructural improvements that will substantially improve the immediate area, as well as recreation opportunities in the sports fields and aquatic center. The site will provide significant amenities for both local residents as well as visiting tourists.

03

01.02: A series of botanical garden rooms and immersive environments explore the ecological zones of Mexico. 03: Program works in tandem with ecological structure.

01

RENAISSANCE PARK
Chattanooga, Tennessee

The Chattanooga **Renaissance Park** incorporates a landscape restoration strategy and stormwater treatment wetland within its larger functioning as an urban park. The park was envisioned as part of the Chattanooga 21st Century Waterfront masterplan, and is sited across the Tennessee River from the 21st Century Waterfront (see *Cultures and Water*). The 23.5-acre site, on the north shore of the river, was a former kitchen appliance factory and the ground was polluted with frit, the waste product of the enameling process. Hargreaves Associates devised a two-fold approach to remediate the site: contain the contaminated soil and clean the stormwater that passes through the site. The contaminated soils on site were treated through containment and geotechnical stabilization. The wetland treats stormwater in an intermittent stream that passes first through the city and then through the site and into the Tennessee River. Before the constructed wetland was built, this created a significant non-source point pollution for the Tennessee River. With the addition of the constructed wetland, the park treats water from a 470-acre catchment from downtown Chattanooga, treating the first flush of pollution during storm events. The design of the wetland consists of gabions fingers, planted with native riparian species, that extend into the wetland and filter the water that circulates through the wetland. Once stormwater passes through the wetland, the filtered water is released into the Tennessee River.

Renaissance Park balances the restoration goals of the site and stormwater filtration with program geared to local families. Using the fill from the wetland excavation, Hargreaves Associates created playful landforms for children.

01

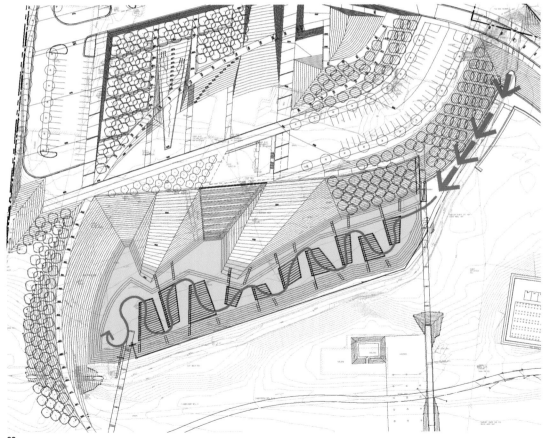

02

The Adventure Playground overlooks the treatment wetland. The park is joined with the 21st Century Waterfront on the other side of the Tennessee through a continuation of the marking of the Trail of Tears through the Renaissance site. The path is constructed as a narrative journey, through fragmented segments of the trail which lead to clearings in the woods. The broken path symbolizes the devastated lives of the Native Americans who were forced westward by the Indian Removal Act of 1830. The clearings in the woods are used by teachers to instruct on the ecology of the riverine forest and the history and significance of the Trail of Tears.

01: Gabions fingers planted with native riparian species extend into the wetland and filter the water that circulates through. **02**: Diagram of stormwater as it moves through the wetland.

03

04

05

01-04: Views of the constructed wetland.
05: A fragmented path through the woods constructs a narrative journey, referencing the Trail of Tears. Clearings in the woods are used by teachers for instruction on the site ecology and history.

LOS ANGELES STATE HISTORIC PARK
Los Angeles, California

Hargreaves Associates is currently developing the design for **Los Angeles State Historic Park** after winning the 2006 competition (see *Competitions*). The design phase expands the key concepts that guided the competition, and rethinks the overall spatial distribution of landscape typologies and program elements. When completed, the park will provide open space in a city that has history of a dearth of public urban open space. The fundamental goals of this urban park are interpretative, ecological and social, expressing

the park as a unique cultural landscape, articulating the interdependencies of its historical context and shifting ecologies in contemporary Los Angeles and activating the urban downtown. As a cultural landscape, the site has acquired accrued meanings throughout history through an assemblage of forces of industry, agriculture, immigration, and ecology. The design for the park interprets the site's sociological history and ecological systems, expressing a burgeoning relationship between the city and the LA River. With the

edge of the park located just 300 feet from the channelized LA River and interest from the communities to reconnect with urban ecologies, Hargreaves Associates is able to engage the reclamation of the river as part of the development of the park.

Hargreaves Associates led the team in development of an interpretive design approach reinforcing multiple aspects of the project, including landscape, architecture and interactive displays, crafting the expression of the park as a cultural landscape and

telling the story of the diverse cultural significance of the site. The park design interprets history and ecology through a range of design elements from inscribed paths to gardens to architectural resource centers. The park presents a narrative approach to site while creating usable programmed spaces for a range of activities.

As the site of early settlement on the LA River, and also the former Southern Pacific Railyard, the site registers a range of events that contributed to the development of Los Angeles and the region.

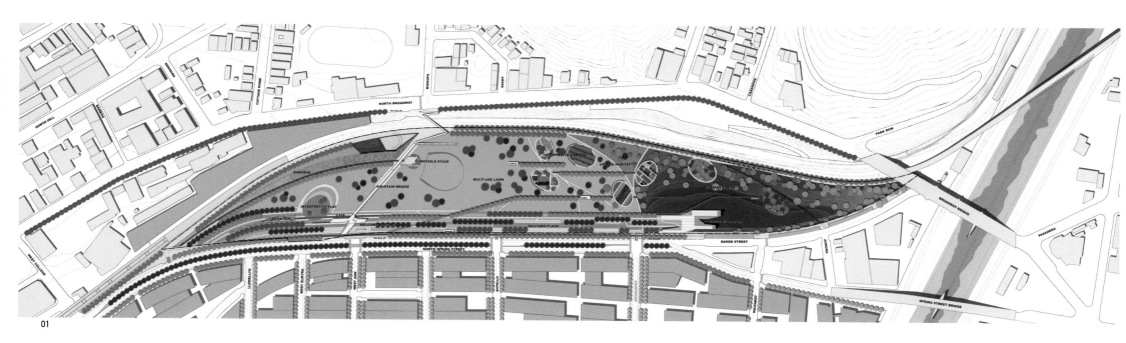

01

02

01: The park engages the reclamation of the LA River as part of its development. 02: The design emphasizes the grain of the historic rail lines. 03: Diagram of water strategies in the park.

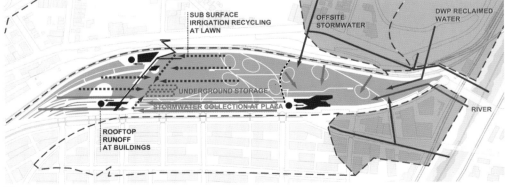

03

01

02

INTERPRETIVE PATHS AND PORTALS

Interpretive elements: shade structure with words/images, storytelling space, words embedded in paths, tabletop

culture

nature

community water industry

COMMUNITY	INDUSTRY	WATER	NATURE	CULTURE
Theme: Recreation LA communities, civic pride, park creation	Theme: History of Place growth, expansion, labor, struggle, progress	Theme: Water cultivation, labor, celebration, renewal	Theme: Environmental Action pre-history, river, habitat, environmental awareness	Theme: People's History arrival, encounter, displacement, celebration, ceremony, diversity, renewal

INTERPRETIVE ARCHITECTURE

broadway bridge

fountain bridge

welcome station

ecology center

WELCOME STATION	FOUNTAIN BRIDGE	ECOLOGY CENTER
orientation map, digital mural, cultural connectivity map, story collection/faces past and present, roof observatory with view sheds	interpretation points for site features and historic bridge, overlook for turntable	urban ecology, la river, agriculture, sustainability, environmental awareness

INTERPRETIVE GARDENS

Interpretive elements: storytelling areas, cycles of seasons, ceremonies, cultivation, words/statistics

FOURTH NATURE	THIRD NATURE	SECOND NATURE	FIRST NATURE
civic/cultural gardens	ceremonial garden, cultural garden	early settlement garden, interactive agriculture, garden grove	l.a. river garden, hyper nature garden

MEDIA ACCESS

Interpretive elements: media access points at park architecture, portals, interpretive gardens, interpretive play area, habitat zones, and archaeological reveals

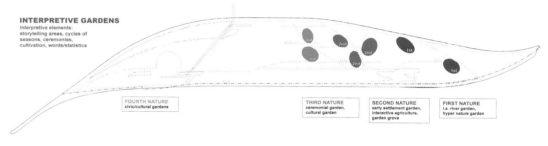

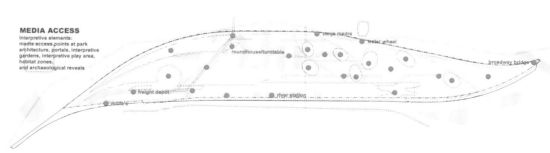

zanja madre

water wheel

roundhouse/turntable

broadway bridge

freight depot

river station

mills

03

04

Known as the Ellis Island of the West, the railyard was the entry point for a massive influx of immigrants to California. Hargreaves Associates references the diverse cultures of Los Angeles through planting strategies that use agricultural and horticultural species from all over the world in ceremonial and cultural interpretive gardens. The site witnessed tragic historical events – where Japanese-Americans were collected to be sent to internment camps during World War II and the Zoot Suit Riots of 1943. The railroad also contributed to the agricultural development of California, efficiently transporting crops. The site's proximity to the

LA River engages the park with the larger ecological systems of the region. Zones of the park recreate the vanished wetland ecologies. Interpretive gardens are ecological, creating habitat; instructional, demonstrating gardening to visitors; and cultural, acting as sites for weddings and parties. The park is poised to interface with a future naturalized LA River, setting the stage to engage the complex ecology of the site and the region.

Hargreaves Associates implement the historic grain of the site, the former rail tracks of the Southern Pacific Railroad, to provide the overall structure for the site. The design activates the entire

Spring Street edge of the park through a long, linear urban plaza that emphasizes the grain of the historic rail lines. A porous edge, this plaza emphasizes connection to downtown Los Angeles. As the downtown core continues to expand, the park's impact will grow in significance as development moves toward the park. Moving into the park, the site transforms from urban edge to open lawn. Across the park (from downtown to the LA River) Hargreaves Associates overlays a gradient framework from the urban to the ecological that determines activity, use, and planting.

01: Program nodes crop up throughout the multi-use lawn, including a performance stage at the Turntable. **02**: The Fountain Bridge tells the story of the site through an engaging structure. **03**: The urban plaza emphasizes connection to downtown Los Angeles. **04**: The park recreates vanished wetland ecologies.

| Camphor tree | Valley Oak | Coast Live Oak | California Black Walnut | Blue Elderberry | Fremont Cottonwood | California Sycamore | White Alder |
| *Cinnamomum camphora* | *Quercus lobata* | *Quercus agrifolia* | *Juglans californica* | *Sambucus mexicana* | *Populus fremontii* | *Platanus racemosa* | *Alnus rhombifolia* |

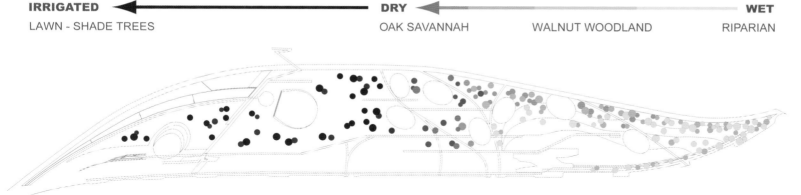

| Lawn | Creeping Wild Rye | Mugwort | Sugar Bush | Fuchsia-flowered Gooseberry | Creeping Snowberry | Pink Hedgenettle | Slender sedge |
| | *Leymus triticoides* | *Artemisia douglasiana* | *Rhus ovat* | *Ribes speciosum* | *Symphoricarpos mollis* | *Stachys bullata* | *Carex praegracilis* |

01

IRRIGATED ← **DRY** ← **WET**

LAWN - SHADE TREES   OAK SAVANNAH   WALNUT WOODLAND   RIPARIAN

02

From the urban plaza, five interpretive paths lead into the park, following the form of switching rail lines, and explore five themes of the site – *community, industry, water, nature* and *culture*. These themes are evoked through design language – words inscribed on paths, shade structures, and at Portals – clearings with moments of rest and instructional gathering spaces. Hargreaves Associates is working with Ralph Appelbaum Associates to structure the interpretive themes of the park and with Michael Maltzan Architects to design the architectural structures in the park including a Welcome Station that greets visitors to the park and provides maps, stories, murals and prospects from which to view the park. The Fountain Bridge tells the story of the site through a structure that can be walked over, viewing the entire site, or below, engaging with a dynamic water feature. The Fountain Bridge connects to the existing Broadway Street, creating another point of access to the northwest. An Ecology Center also acts as a community center, providing space and resources for the ecological program as well as the more general needs of the community. Within the arrangement of site program, there is an openness of circulation in the main body of the site. The design strikes a balance between directed circulation system and expanses of open space where free movement is encouraged. Program nodes crop up throughout the multi-use lawn, including interpretive gardens, play areas, and a performance stage at the Turntable, the exact location where train cars were rotated at the terminus of the rail line.

01: The agricultural gardens include early settlement crops and fruit trees that are cultivated throughout California. **02**: Shade structures incorporate the themes from the interpretive paths.

Planting strategies across the site reinforce the gradient structure of the park from urban to ecological. The design of the park creates a range of interpretive gardens from the horticultural to the cultural to the agricultural to the ecological. Horticultural garden collections will be the sites of ceremonies. The agricultural gardens include early settlement crops and fruit trees – oranges, lemons and almonds – that are cultivated throughout California. The food crops grown on the site will be used at the park's restaurant. In areas designated as *Hyper Nature,* plantings will include non-native plants that thrive in the Los Angeles climate and have dramatic visual affect. Closest to the LA River, Hargreaves Associates reintroduce the native wetland ecologies.

Los Angeles State Historic Park is poised for the future. The park's relationship to downtown LA will increase over time, as the urban core of downtown grows toward the park. The park design anticipates the merging of the urban fabric into the park site, negotiated by the linear plaza across the downtown edge. To facilitate this, Hargreaves Associates are reaching into the city, creating pedestrian friendly streets leading to the park. The park design incorporates bike storage within the park, and bike lanes leading to the park, laying the groundwork for alternative transportation. At the river's edge, the design encourages the naturalization of the LA River. Hargreaves Associates are actively planning for the first step in the recovery of the LA River. Future phases of the park will merge these two key open space systems and link the park into the greater ecological systems of Los Angeles. The park interprets history by anticipating a future of rich urban open space and a reclaimed relationship to its natural systems.

FIRST NATURE
"unmediated, untouched, and primal, in reality or imagination"

SECOND NATURE
"brought into being by deliberate and physical human agency"

THIRD NATURE
"involves a specific intention of the creator to make a space more beautiful, noting that the quest for beauty is further rooted in a quest for the conjuring of a sense of aesthetic pleasure"

Quotes from *Greater Perfections - the Practice of Garden Theory* by John Dixon Hunt

LA RIVER GARDEN
Plants native to the Los Angeles River corridor representing the land as it existed before settlement.

HYPER NATURE GARDEN
Plants native to Southern California, with some non-native flowering perennials to attract a diversity of birds and butterflies.

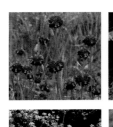

EARLY SETTLEMENT GARDEN
Plants used by local Gabrielino/ Tongva and early Spanish settlers for food, medicine, clothing, and building.

INTERACTIVE AGRICULTURE GARDEN
L.A. region grain and vegetable crops common in the Statehood Era (1848-1876) - a garden for urban agriculture focused on education through hands on experience.

GARDEN GROVE
L.A. region fruit and nut crops common in the Statehood Era (1848-1876).

CEREMONIAL GARDEN
A garden featuring plants used in the ceremonies, events and festivals of the diverse communities of the LA region.

CULTURAL GARDEN
A garden celebrating the diversity of garden plants and gardenhistory in Los Angeles, rich in color and texture.

LONDON OLYMPICS 2012
London, United Kingdom

The landscape at the **London 2012 Olympic Park** is designed specifically for a distinct life during Olympic Games and in a second incarnation, afterwards as a *Legacy Park* for a developing East London. In their design for a new major urban park, Hargreaves Associates draw on the extremely rich heritage of large parks throughout London. As a 21st century version of the classic London park, the Olympic park will provide many amenities of the traditional large urban park with sweeping lawns, a promenade, and gardens of display. These traditional typologies are updated in the park with the most current green technologies for flood control and habitat creation.

The site for the Olympic Games is on the banks of the River Lea, an industrial river that winds through the heart of East London. The Lea forms part of a post-industrial navigation network that provides an arterial waterway through East London. The industrial character of the river caused it and the entire East End to be heavily bombed in WWII, leaving an enduring quality of urban neglect. Construction of the park revealed an unexploded bomb that required a controlled detonation. With the land on the banks of the Lea polluted from its past industrial use, an aggressive environmental remediation is required as a first stage of construction. The cleanup, managed by the Olympic Delivery Authority (ODA) entails stripping the top level of soil, cleaning it through a baking process and soil washing, and then returning it to the site. Hargreaves Associates designed the grading of the site in concert with this procedure.

01: The site for the Olympic Games is on the banks of the River Lea, an industrial river that winds through the heart of East London. **02**: The plan for the Olympic Games with venues.

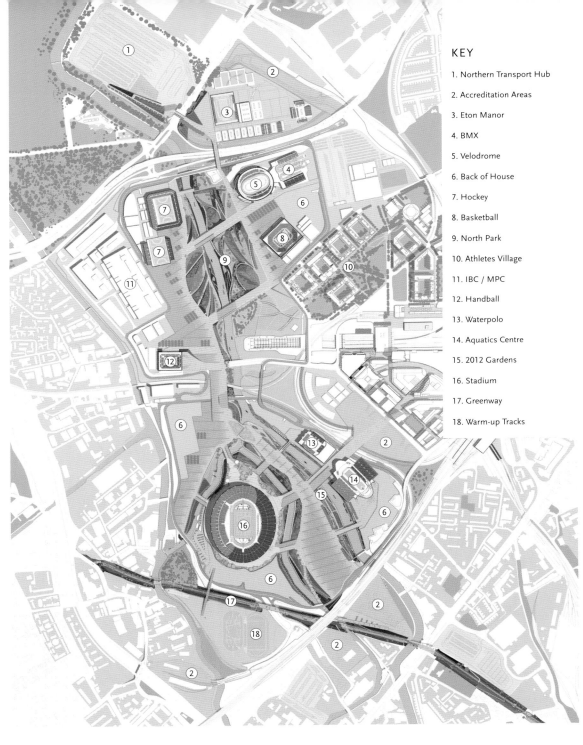

KEY

1. Northern Transport Hub
2. Accreditation Areas
3. Eton Manor
4. BMX
5. Velodrome
6. Back of House
7. Hockey
8. Basketball
9. North Park
10. Athletes Village
11. IBC / MPC
12. Handball
13. Waterpolo
14. Aquatics Centre
15. 2012 Gardens
16. Stadium
17. Greenway
18. Warm-up Tracks

Games Mode

01

NORTH PARK - Layered Park Components

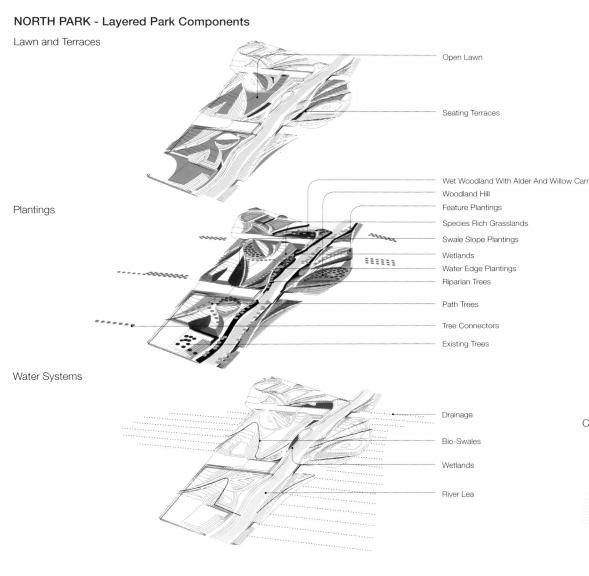

Lawn and Terraces

— Open Lawn

— Seating Terraces

Plantings

— Wet Woodland With Alder And Willow Carr
— Woodland Hill
— Feature Plantings
— Species Rich Grasslands
— Swale Slope Plantings
— Wetlands
— Water Edge Plantings
— Riparian Trees
— Path Trees
— Tree Connectors
— Existing Trees

Water Systems

— Drainage
— Bio-Swales
— Wetlands
— River Lea

Landforms

The construction of the park emphasizes the renewal of the River Lea. Hargreaves Associates actualize this transformation of the landscape by reshaping the river's edge. Currently in a deep channel condition, the walls will be removed, reintroducing gentle banks to the river, naturalizing the river and creating a more generous adjoining open space pathway. The sloped section to the river will vary along its length, reflecting adjacent uses. The banks of the river will be engineered to withstand flooding, regulating the flow of water through the entire park. In the more urbanized areas of the Park, steeper banks and promenades will reflect this more urban condition.

Around the newly constructed river's edge, surrounding Parklands, sculpted into areas of prospect and refuge, will provide a figure of landscape for the Olympic site. The Parklands are divided into North and South areas, emphasizing habitat and ecology in the northern part and a more urban setting to the south. A Concourse will run through the entire Park, creating a unifying plaza and circulation scheme for the Olympic venues, similar to the *Red Move* at Sydney.

Circulation

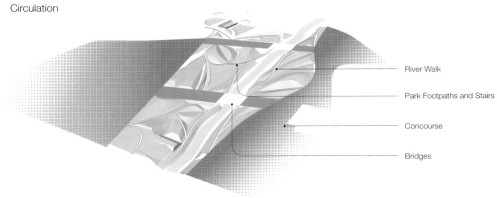

— River Walk
— Park Footpaths and Stairs
— Concourse
— Bridges

01: The landscape is designed specifically for a distinct life during Olympic Games and in a second incarnation, afterwards as a *Legacy Park* for a developing East London. **02:** The north area of the park emphasizes habitat and ecology.

During the Games, temporary outdoor screens with seating areas will be erected off of the Concourse on open lawns with gentle topography, allowing visitors to watch televised parts of the Games along the riverbanks. The southern part of the park sites the core of stadiums and other sporting centers during the Olympic Games. A series of gardens in this area emphasize a cultural expression of the British love of plants from around the world. Inspired in part by Victorian pleasure gardens, Hargreaves Associates have designed a system of gardens that celebrates the multicultural nature of the Olympics while tracing the journey of Britain's plant collectors through four climatic zones – Western Europe, the Mediterranean, and Asia Minor; The Temperate Americas; the Southern Hemisphere, South Africa, Australia and New Zealand; and Temperate Asia, including montane China, Japan and the Himalayas. These plant collections will be displayed in garden zones between the Aquatics Center and the Olympic Stadium and will be maintained after the Games to provide a continuing draw for regional visitors into the park.

Games Mode

Transformation Mode

Games Mode

Transformation Mode

Games Mode

Transformation Mode

After the conclusion of the Games, the park will enter a transformation phase making the new park accessible to the public as soon as possible after the Games. The transformation removes the temporary infrastructure throughout the park, deconstructs the temporary venues and downsizes the stadiums, converting them into new uses that will serve the neighboring communities and future developments in the neighborhoods. The Parklands will also transform, shifting their focus to the surrounding neighborhoods and their second life as a significant large park in East London, part of the system of great English parks. The *Legacy Park* will take specific measures to fully integrate into the existing neighborhoods as well as facilitate the development of industrial areas by establishing a significant public amenity for the district.

01

01: The Olympic Stadium.
02,03: The plaza around the Olympic Stadium, during and after the Games.

02

03

01

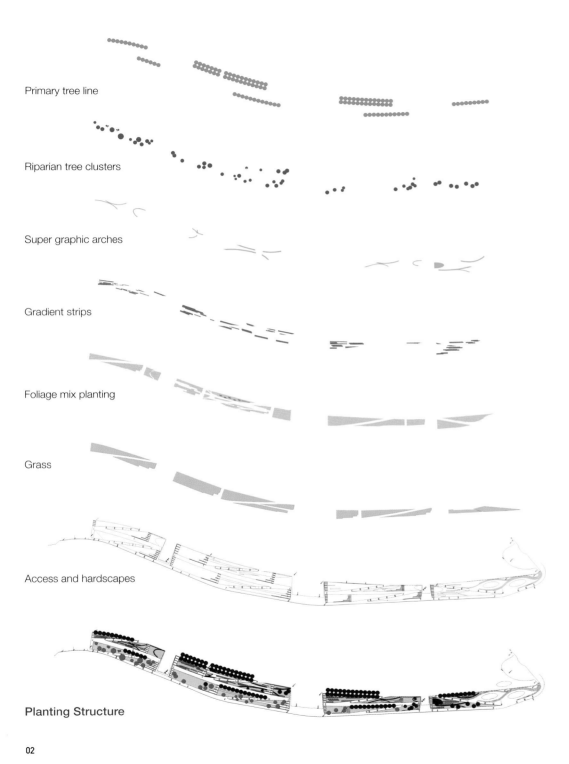

Primary tree line

Riparian tree clusters

Super graphic arches

Gradient strips

Foliage mix planting

Grass

Access and hardscapes

Planting Structure

02

As a linear park, organized around the River Lea, the post-Games park will have a different character than Central London's Hyde Park, and the other centuries' old parks of the city, but large, robust and pliant, the *Legacy Park* will be able to support 21st century urban life appropriate to the developing neighborhood. Linear pathways of recreation will course through the neighborhoods, with extensions into local streets. The northern part of the park will continue its focus on ecology, supporting native habitat on over 100 of the 250 total acres of parkland. The southern areas, around the converted Olympic venues, will retain the social, urban and festival nature established during the Games. The plaza will remain and provide infrastructure for neighborhood activities such as markets and festivals. Olympic venues converted to community centers and sporting centers will support the local communities. The community will also continue to make use of the cafés constructed for the Games.

The Olympic Park creates a lasting legacy for London. It creates a heroic, 21st century incarnation of the British Park for the international event, as well as a lasting amenity. During the Games, the park will serve as a symbol of Great Britain. Afterwards, the Park will provide vital services and an open space structure for a changing district, working hand in hand with civic development authorities.

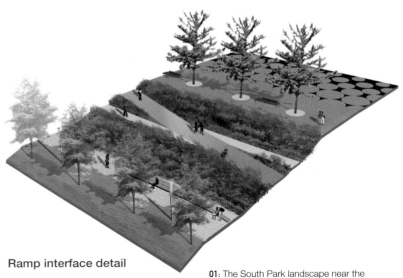

Ramp interface detail

03

01: The South Park landscape near the Stadium. 02: The planting structure of the South Park. 03: Plaza, circulation, and planting create the landscape structure.

01

01-02: A series of gardens in this area emphasize a cultural expression of the British love of plants from around the world.

TEMPERATE ASIA, PARTICULARLY MONTANE CHINA, JAPAN AND THE HIMALAYAS
C19th C20th

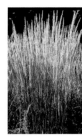

PLANTING TYPOLOGIES - KEY CATEGORIES:

TREES & SHRUB SPECIES

FORMAL CLIPPED HEDGING

BOLD FOLIAGE STRIPS

FLOWERING PERENNIALS

DENSE VERTICAL PLANTING STRIPS

TRANSPARENT / TALL EMERGENT PLANTING STRIPS

THE SOUTHERN HEMISPHERE, SOUTH AFRICA, AUSTRALIA, NEW ZEALAND
C18th early C19th

TREES & SHRUB SPECIES

FORMAL CLIPPED HEDGING

'FIELD' PLANTING

FLOWERING PERENNIALS

DENSE VERTICAL PLANTING STRIPS

TRANSPARENT / TALL EMERGENT PLANTING STRIPS

BULB STRIPS

TEMPERATE AMERICAS
C17th C18th

TREES & SHRUB SPECIES

FORMAL CLIPPED HEDGING

'FIELD' PLANTING

FLOWERING PERENNIALS

DENSE VERTICAL PLANTING STRIPS

TRANSPARENT / TALL EMERGENT PLANTING STRIPS

BULB STRIPS

WESTERN EUROPE, THE MEDITERRANEAN AND ASIA MINOR
post 1400 AD

TREES & SHRUB SPECIES

FORMAL CLIPPED HEDGING

'FIELD' PLANTING

FLOWERING PERENNIALS

DENSE VERTICAL PLANTING STRIPS

TRANSPARENT / TALL EMERGENT PLANTING STRIPS

BULB STRIPS

WALTHAM FOREST

STRATFORD CITY

HACKNEY WICK

FISH ISLAND

OLD FORD

CITY MILL

RIVER LEE
NAVIGATION

BOW

PPR Transformation Boundary

Existing Development

Key Connectors

Future Development Parcels

01

Designed as a place of resilience, the park continues to perform long after the Olympics are over, designed to act as a major factor in the urban revitalization of the East End. The park performs for the community, aiding development and facilitating recreation, and performs for the local ecology, improving habitat and the environment.

These urban park sites vary in scale and scope, but share common threads, creating unique cultural landscape appropriate to their singular communities. In these works, Hargreaves Associates refine strategies of narrative and interpretation, program, and sustainability. Through projects like Discovery Green, Hargreaves Associates developed new strategies of layering program, creating multiplicity and density within a small site. At LA State Historic Park and Acuario Xochimilco, program is treated on a larger scale, with cohesive overall spatial organization creating flexible public space. Through the projects, Hargreaves Associates pursue sustainability to rethink urban infrastructure, using landscape structures to treat stormwater and remediate brownfields. These urban parks move beyond modernism and its later missteps, rejecting a stiff formalism but unafraid of form or bold ideas. The parks act in manifold ways, revitalizing faltering neighborhoods, reinforcing history, and reintroducing ecology to the urban environment, ultimately creating a sense of place through design that both invents and interprets.

02

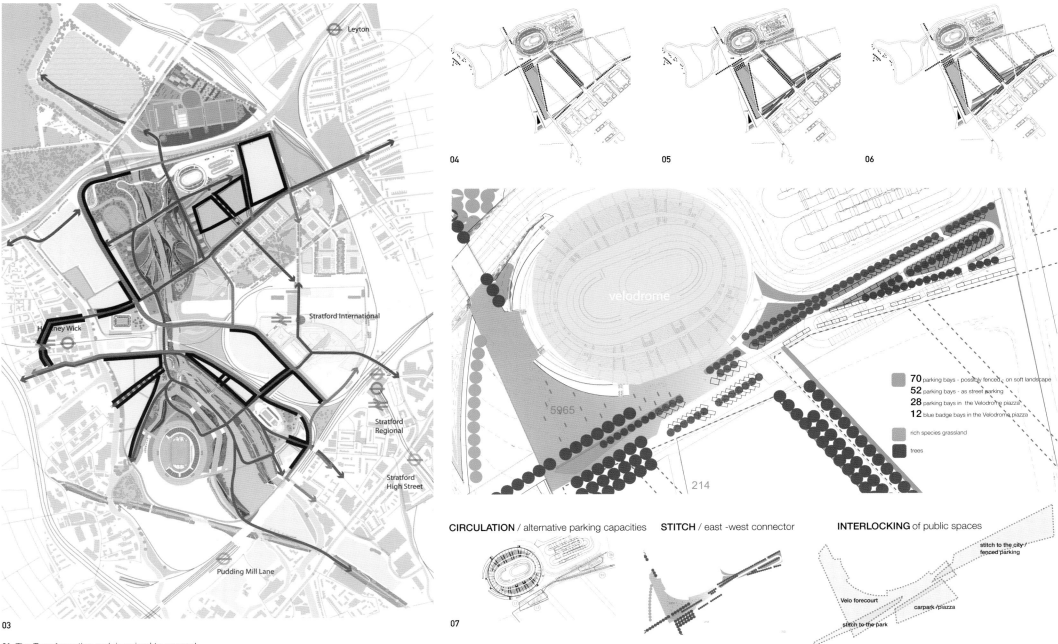

04   05   06

CIRCULATION / alternative parking capacities   **STITCH** / east -west connector   **INTERLOCKING** of public spaces

07

70 parking bays - possibly fenced - on soft landscape
52 parking bays - as street parking
28 parking bays in the Velodrome piazza
12 blue badge bays in the Velodrome piazza

rich species grassland

trees

velodrome

5965

214

stitch to the city / fenced parking

Velo forecourt   carpark /plazza

stitch to the park

03

01: The Transformation park is poised to connect
to surrounding neighborhoods. **02:** The Stitch landscape
strategy joins new development into the existing park.
03: Circulation through the park emphasizes neighborhood
connections. **04-06:** Stitch connections anticipate multiple
future development goals **07:** The Velopark Stitch forms
a linear green connection between the Transformation
Park and the communities to the east.

COMPETITIONS

ORANGE COUNTY GREAT PARK
Los Angeles, California

Competitions are a key tool that allows Hargreaves Associates to advance the conceptual work of the firm. Over the duration of ongoing work, on projects for clients, on research for books and classes taught, half-formed notions collect unimplemented, too imprecise, or perhaps too audacious to be followed through. As time passes, the fragments begin to find clarity and focus, coalescing around a bold idea. The competition provides the opportunity to fully develop these fledgling ideas. Often, those ideas find their way from competitions to real projects, and back again to competitions, with the firm always searching for the next step in its development of landscape theory and practice. Concepts explored in one competition find fruition in a later project. Implemented ideas perform in one project, are adjusted to the next permutation, and lead to the next body of ideas. Competitions also are a way that landscape architects communicate with each other, actualizing designs that express conceptual approaches to the range of contemporary landscape issues. The 1982 Paris Parc de la Villette competition and the 1999 Downsview Park competition in Toronto are prime examples of how competitions shape the thinking of the entire field. In this volume, the Orange County Great Park competition allowed firms to explore the very large park. In the Governor's Island competition, firms re-conceptualized the contemporary, ultra-urban park. In competitions of this caliber, all the entrants shape the discourse of the profession.

01: The Los Angeles park is on 4000 acres on the site of a former Marine Corps air station. **02:** The design creates a framework for park-making that is both site specific and adaptable.

01

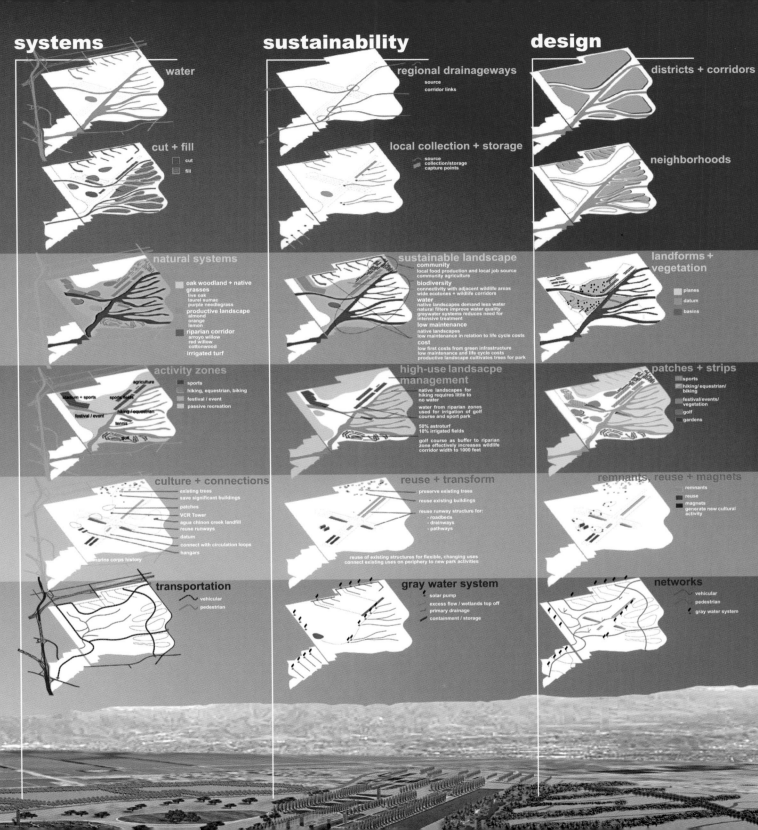

systems

sustainability

design

WATER influences the future and fate of Orange County Great Park. Water will shape the conceptual framework for the park's design, the physical framework for its function, and the programmatic framework for its use. By embracing the condition and implications of water within the park as well as beyond its boundaries, Orange County will create a meaningful, dynamic, and inspirational place that is unique to this site and emblematic of our time.

With water as the ultimate idea and tool, we look to five "constituencies" – the building blocks of design and program that will generate spaces of meaning and beauty within the park itself - nature, activity, culture, infrastructure, and sustainability.

NATURE is the palette. Ten thousand trees cultivated on-site will provide shade for visitors and habitat for wildlife, cooling the water and cleaning the air. From native grasslands to irrigated fields, a variety of landscape textures, each with its particular dependency on water and resultant management strategy, will be introduced or restored in the park.

ACTIVITY populates the park. Orange County Great Park will be a platform for myriad activities to attract visitors and to cultivate communities of different kinds. The park will respond to the needs of every neighborhood, supporting community health through active recreation.

CULTURE enriches experience. The park's multiple pasts, inscribed in the remnants that remain, will be unearthed and transformed to stimulate new creative undertakings. Museums, gardens, festivals, and memorials will provide art for all in cultural districts that preserve the richness of the region.

INFRASTRUCTURE gives flexible limits. Systems which choreograph the movement of pedestrians, vehicles, water, and wildlife across the site establish a flexible foundation for all future development.

systems column labels

water

cut + fill
- cut
- fill

natural systems
- oak woodland + native grasses
  - live oak
  - laurel sumac
  - purple needlegrass
- productive landscape
  - almond
  - orange
  - lemon
- riparian corridor
  - arroyo willow
  - red willow
  - cottonwood
- irrigated turf

activity zones
- sports
- hiking, equestrian, biking
- festival / event
- passive recreation

agriculture
stadium + sports
sports field
festival / event
hiking / equestrian
tennis
golf

culture + connections
- existing trees
- save significant buildings
- patches
- VCR Tower
- agua chinon creek landfill
- reuse runways
- datum
- connect with circulation loops
- hangars

marine corps history

transportation
- vehicular
- pedestrian

sustainability column labels

regional drainageways
- source
- corridor links

local collection + storage
- source
- collection/storage
- capture points

sustainable landscape
- **community**
  local food production and local job source
  community agriculture
- **biodiversity**
  connectivity with adjacent wildlife areas
  wide ecotones + wildlife corridors
- **water**
  native landscapes demand less water
  natural filters improve water quality
  greywater systems reduces need for intensive treatment
- **low maintence**
  native landscapes
  low maintenance in relation to life cycle costs
- **cost**
  low first costs from green infrastructure
  low maintenance and life cycle costs
  productive landscape cultivates trees for park

high-use landsacpe management
native landscapes for hiking requires little to no water
water from riparian zones used for irrigation of golf course and sport park
50% astroturf
10% irrigated fields
golf course as buffer to riparian zone effectively increases wildlife corridor width to 1000 feet

reuse + transform
- preserve existing trees
- reuse existing buildings
- reuse runway structure for:
  - roadbeds
  - drainways
  - pathways

reuse of existing structures for flexible, changing uses
connect existing uses on periphery to new park activities

gray water system
- solar pump
- excess flow / wetlands top off
- primary drainage
- containment / storage

design column labels

districts + corridors

neighborhoods

landforms + vegetation
- planes
- datum
- basins

patches + strips
- sports
- hiking/ equestrian/ biking
- festival/events/ vegetation
- golf
- gardens

remnants, reuse + magnets
- remnants
- reuse
- magnets
- generate new cultural activity

networks
- vehicular
- pedestrian
- gray water system

The **Orange County Great Park** competition advances ideas of process and ecological habitat in the large, regional park. The competition asked for proposals that would create a park for greater Los Angeles, 4000 acres built on the site of the former El Toro Marine Corps Air Station. For Hargreaves Associates, this came on the heels of researching *Large Parks*, co-edited by George Hargreaves and Julia Czerniak, a book that compiles essays on approaches to the world's largest parks, greater than 500 acres[1]. In the book George Hargreaves presents an essay that examines the world's key large parks from a designer's perspective, gaining an understanding of how past use, landscape typology and program create resilient places that support urban life. The competition for Orange County allowed the firm to implement these lessons learned in a contemporary park, with entirely different maintenance regimes than those offered by the Royal Parks of Britain, or the exquisite gardens of Le Nôtre. In the competition entry for Orange County, Hargreaves Associates explore a three-fold design strategy – the physical organization of space and program, the design of ecological systems, and a flexible phasing plan – in order to create a robust park that is responsive to an open-ended future.

At Orange County, Hargreaves Associates take a pragmatic approach to the palimpsest, re-using the structures of the airfield for compatible landscape uses. At the scale of the large park, an ecological scale, site specificity is a strategy of logic. Using the network of existing runways and hangars as a substructure, the design creates a framework for the new park, finding compatible uses for the sublayers of the site. This adaptive re-use creates a built-in site specificity to the landscape, as the new productive landscape is placed only where it can be sustained. Existing buildings are re-used as flexible nodes for new park activities – orchards, gardens and sports fields, and the runways are converted into basins for storing water, and a new system of pathways, roadways and parking.

01: The park incorporates irrigated areas for productive agriculture.
02: Water is channeled above ground through lush riparian corridors.
03: The flexible infrastructure develops over time, adaptable to future circumstances.

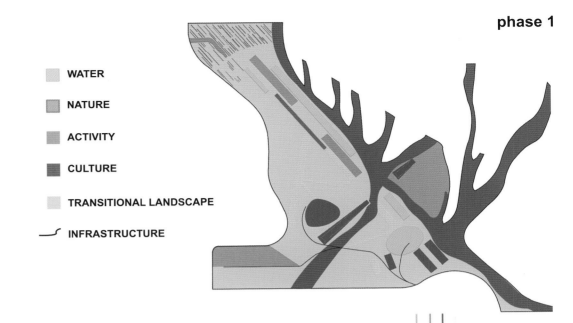

WATER

NATURE

ACTIVITY

CULTURE

TRANSITIONAL LANDSCAPE

INFRASTRUCTURE

phase 2

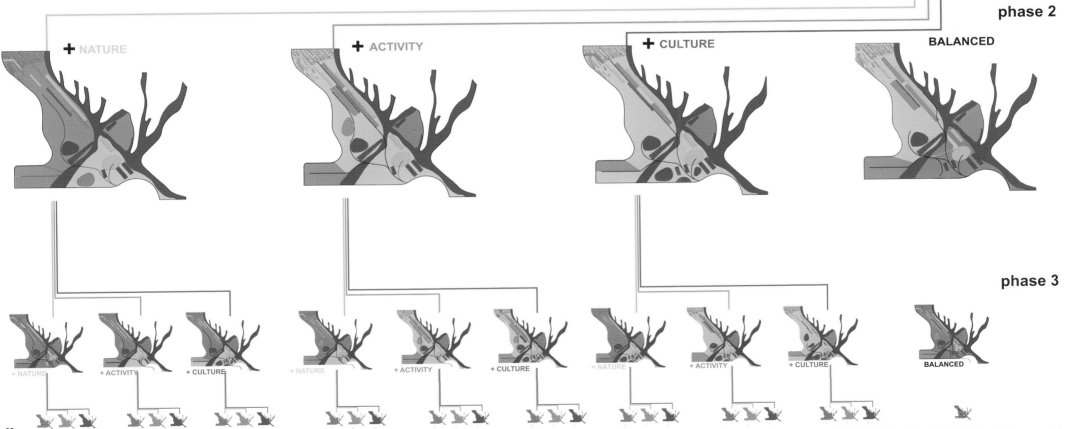

+ NATURE

+ ACTIVITY

+ CULTURE

BALANCED

phase 3

+ NATURE

+ ACTIVITY

+ CULTURE

+ NATURE

+ ACTIVITY

+ CULTURE

+ NATURE

+ ACTIVITY

+ CULTURE

BALANCED

01

01: The design uses the network of existing runways and hangars as a substructure. 02: Irrigated *patches* contain different types of cultural and recreational programs. 03: Existing buildings are re-used as flexible nodes for new park activities.

This framework bleeds through the surface layer of Oak Grassland, the native ecological habitat that dominates the site. This ecological type is well suited to the flat, dry conditions of the site, but is not compatible with recreational use, which would destroy the habitat. In order to facilitate both ecological diversity and recreation the design implements two strategies. The first is a water strategy that creates a drainage system through the park, channeling water above ground through lush riparian corridors. The linear quality of the corridors creates opportunities for recreational trails through the corridors, creating a multifunction infrastructural and recreational system. The water carried through the riparian corridors eventually leads to the airstrip basins that collect the water for irrigation.

This water is used in the second strategy, *patches*, areas within the Oak Grassland habitat that are irrigated and made suitable for recreation. The *patch* system is key to a unique phasing strategy that both builds out the park over time, but also remains open to change as the park develops, incorporating another layer of flexibility into the design. The patches contain different types of cultural and recreational programs. As the park develops, if the community feels that they need additional theater space, a patch devoted to event spaces can be created, likewise for arts and science, history and play themes. The patch is designed as a platform for future activity and programmatic richness. Each area has irrigation and a way to plug into the overall infrastructure network, and is developed over time with necessity, adaptable to future circumstances.

02

03

With this flexibility and public generated program, the design creates a formula for park-making that is both site specific and adaptable. Further, with a proposal that reconciles recreation with ecological habitat, and provides a clear framework of built structures, Hargreaves Associates distinguish the design from proposals that favor an open-ended ecological strategy with little regard for the integration of program and human needs. With the proposal for Orange County, the firm looked to the great large parks of history, which were formed over hundreds of years and continue to provide vital services to their regions. From this example the firm deployed concrete strategies that create richness and complexity, facilitating the same kind of long-term adaptability and resilience.

01

EAST DARLING HARBOUR
Sydney, Australia

01: The urban design scheme privileges the dramatic
waterfront context, unifying landscape with built form.
02: Botanical strips of tall trees, native to Sydney,
enclose sports fields.

In the competition for **East Darling Harbour** in Sydney,
Australia, Hargreaves Associates and Morphosis architects
created an urban design scheme that emphasizes urban
systems, unifying landscape with built form, privileging the
dramatic waterfront context, and creating water infrastructure
that addresses local conditions of drought. The proposal creates
an urban design that posits an integral open space system
across the entire waterfront to site built form and landscape
program. A long, skinny site, this verticality is broken
down by horizontal strips that take the form of landscape
– botanical strips of tall trees, native to Sydney, that enclose
sports fields – as well as built structures – the retail/residential
buildings that also enclose open space. In this way, landscape
as well as architecture takes on the role of figure on the site,

and the basic figure ground relationships move past the
traditional corollary of landscape = ground and architecture
= figure to a place where landscape slips freely between
figure and ground.

The scheme proposes a sub-structure of open space that
supports landscape program as well as built structures.
The built structures are separated into two nodes – an office
complex at one end of the site and a retail and residential
complex at the other end of the site. Open space is consolidated
at the peninsula, with buildings placed back from the water's
edge. This open space preserves the open viewsheds out
to harbor for both recreational uses and the built structures.
Parks are interspersed across the site.

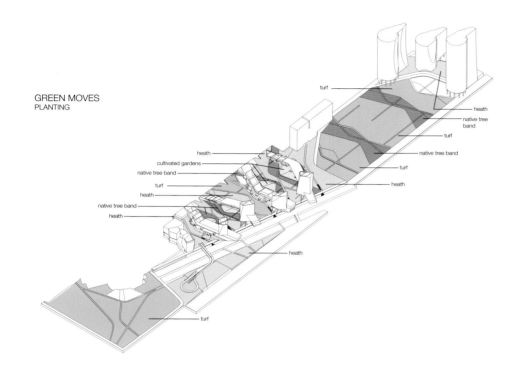

GREEN MOVES
PLANTING

turf

heath

native tree band

turf

native tree band

heath

cultivated gardens

native tree band

turf

heath

native tree band

heath

heath

turf

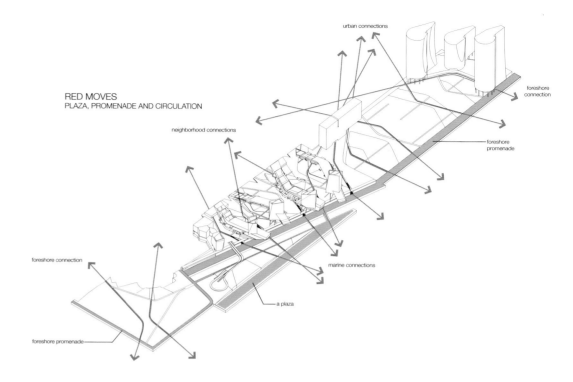

RED MOVES
PLAZA, PROMENADE AND CIRCULATION

urban connections

foreshore connection

neighborhood connections

foreshore promenade

foreshore connection

marine connections

foreshore promenade

a plaza

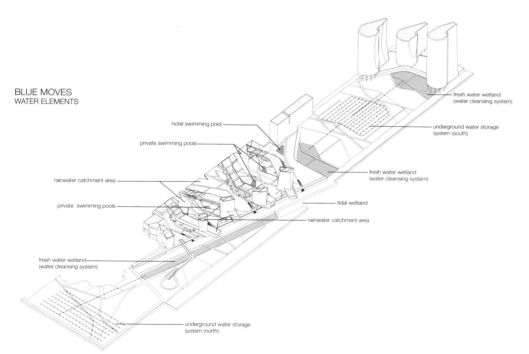

BLUE MOVES
WATER ELEMENTS

fresh water wetland
(water cleansing system)

hotel swimming pool

underground water storage
system (south)

private swimming pools

fresh water wetland
(water cleansing system)

rainwater catchment area

tidal wetland

private swimming pools

rainwater catchment area

fresh water wetland
(water cleansing system)

underground water storage
system (north)

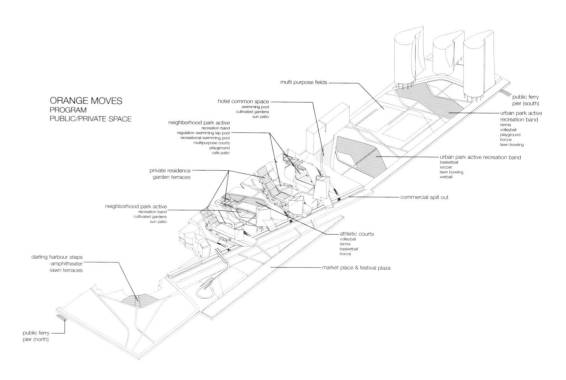

ORANGE MOVES
PROGRAM
PUBLIC/PRIVATE SPACE

multi purpose fields

public ferry
pier (south)

hotel common space
swimming pool
cultivated gardens
sun patio

urban park active
recreation band
tennis
volleyball
playground
bocce
lawn bowling

neighborhood park active
recreation band
regulation swimming lap pool
recreational swimming pool
multipurpose courts
playground
cafe patio

private residence
garden terraces

urban park active recreation band
basketball
soccer
lawn bowling
wetball

neighborhood park active
recreation band
cultivated gardens
sun patio

commercial spill out

athletic courts
volleyball
tennis
basketball
bocce

darling harbour steps
-amphitheater
-lawn terraces

market place & festival plaza

public ferry
pier (north)

Across the entire site the open space is further broken down into park systems that interface with the adjacent neighborhoods. The City Park provides the active programming of the sports fields. The High Street Park gives access to the waterfront to the adjacent neighborhoods by providing a transition point across a grade change. The Peninsula Park juts into the Bay and creates a large open space to celebrate the setting and host large city-wide festivals. The design incorporates a natural rock outcrop on the peninsula as a sculpted amphitheater. The entire built structure of the site integrates water infrastructure. Rooftops provide catchment areas for water collection, which is stored under the large open spaces. Freshwater wetlands cleanse this water, which is then used on site for irrigation in the dry months. This urban design scheme integrates landscape and architecture on a more human scale than the grand scale of landscape urbanism. Embedded infrastructure strengthens the performance of the landscape to create a social space for work, play and life.

01, 02: The urban design posits an integral open space system across the entire waterfront site. **03:** A natural rock outcrop on the peninsula forms a sculpted amphitheater.

01

02

03

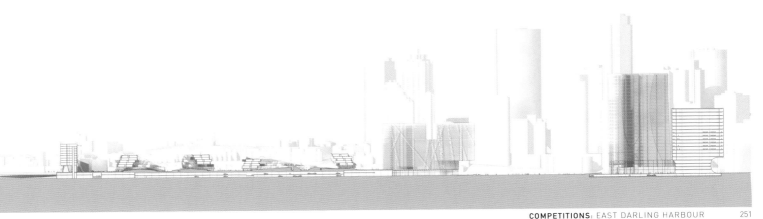

01

The competition for the **Los Angeles State Historic Park,** like Governor's Island, takes into account the cultural specificities and history of a major metropolis. Hargreaves Associates, working with architect Michael Maltzan and interpretive planner Ralph Appelbaum, won this competition sponsored by the California State Parks Foundation (with a grant from the Annenberg Foundation) in 2006. The existing site conditions and historical breadth of the site is fully discussed in the *Urban Parks* section, which shows how the design changes from the competition phase.

On the site of the former Southern Pacific River Station railyard, the thirty-two-acre site is strongly rooted in the history

of migration into Los Angeles, significant to the myriad immigrant communities of Los Angeles. At the same time, the site's location next to the Los Angeles River, prompted Hargreaves Associates to legitimize and enhance the ecological significance of the channelized LA River. A wholly urban condition, the overall park framework negotiates a transition from the urban downtown to a naturalized ecology as the park approaches the LA River. The urban zone emphasizes event spaces and didactic interpretations of the history of the site. This urban character gradually transitions to a naturalized character, supporting native wetland ecologies. The competition proposal includes a strategy to gradually naturalize the LA River channel and incorporate the undulating river flows into the park.

fauna bridge

Solano canyon bridge

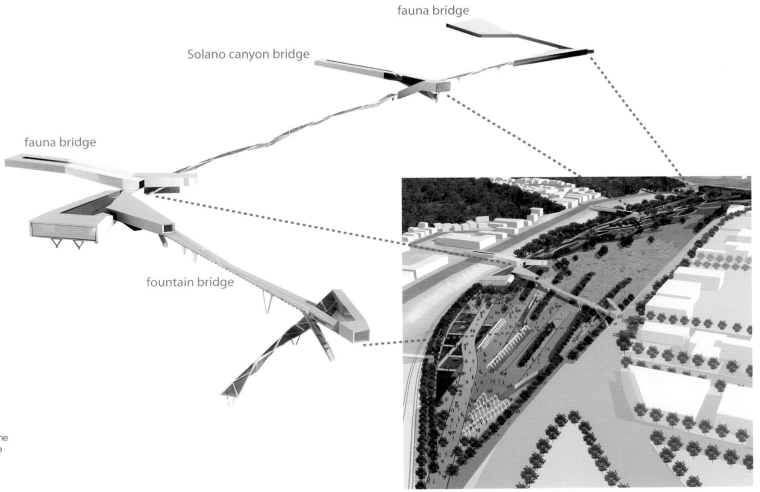

fauna bridge

fountain bridge

01: The urban zone emphasizes event spaces and didactic interpretations of the history of the site. 02: Landscape and architecture reinforce the interpretive message. 03: Open lawns create flexible park space. 04: Botanical garden collections pay tribute to the immigrant communities of Los Angeles.

02

03

04

The interpretive gardens and open lawns create the transition from the urban edge to the wetland ecology and river edge. In the competition phase, this phasing occurs from southwest to northeast, while in the schematic design phase the urban edge is defined along the entire southeastern edge.

Hargreaves Associates use the existing rail lines to create an overall grain for the park and a reoccurring design motif. Site elements are expressed through the patterns of the rail, which forms a modular strip system into which program can be inserted, including farmer's market tents, fountains and playgrounds. Running across the site is a conceptual timeline of site history, following the threads of narrative that formed the site and working to engage visitors with the politics of the site. Hargreaves Associates worked closely with Ralph Appelbaum Associates and Michael Maltzan Architects to create strong links between landscape and architecture that reinforce the interpretive message. The design team developed a Fountain Bridge for the competition that links the Café and Visitors Center creating a dynamic relationship between landscape and architecture on the site, heightening the experience of the plaza space. The competition for the Los Angeles State Historic Park sought to create an interpretive, narrative based explication of site with contemporary significance. The design develops a broad swath of transition from urban to a reclaimed naturalism, unified by the history of the site.

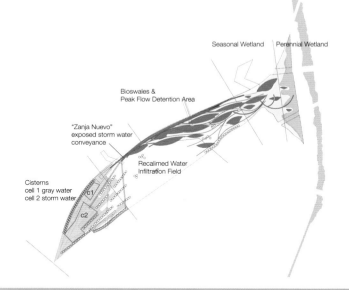

Seasonal Wetland Perennial Wetland

Bioswales &
Peak Flow Detention Area

"Zanja Nuevo"
exposed storm water
conveyance

Recalimed Water
Infiltration Field

Cisterns
cell 1 gray water
cell 2 storm water

c1

c2

01

02

01: Park structures facilitate evening film screenings.
02: The interpretive gardens and open lawns create the transition from the urban edge to the wetland ecology and river edge.
03: The Fountain Bridge engages visitors.

River Scenarios

No change in channel

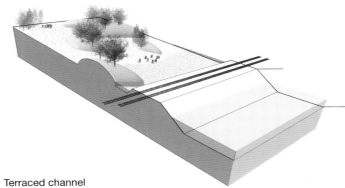

Terraced channel

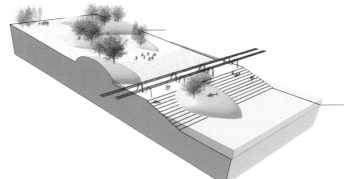

Soft channel

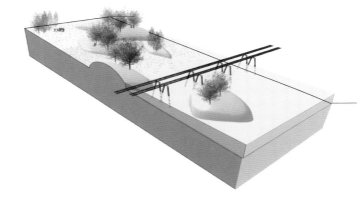

03

01

GOVERNOR'S ISLAND
New York, New York

Region
x 10000

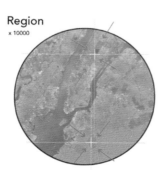

New York City looks inward at its Parks

City
x 1000

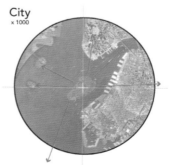

Governors Island looks outward to the City

Park
x 100

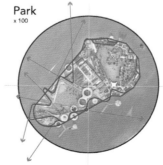

Summer Park marks an Edge and a Center

Building
x 10

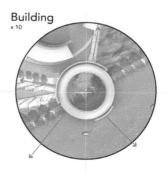

Buildings look outward, provide amenities inward

02

The 2007 **Governor's Island** Competition attracted the attention of the entire field of landscape architecture and architecture. Hargreaves Associates was among five shortlisted teams that produced full proposals for the park, exhibited at the Center For Architecture in New York in the summer of 2007. At a broad level, the firm used its research from the *Large Parks* book in order to think strategically about a richly programmed park that also offers a diverse landscape experience. As a New York City Park, the design proposal looked at Governor's Island in terms of the New York urban experience, as well as in relationship with the entire New York City Parks system.

01: The park emphasizes the view outwards to the city, inverting the typical New York City park experience. **02**: The northern part of the site is maintained as an historic district, with 150 acres of new parkland at the southern end of the site. **03**: The park is organized by a perimeter promenade, constructed views, architecture, and landscape typologies.

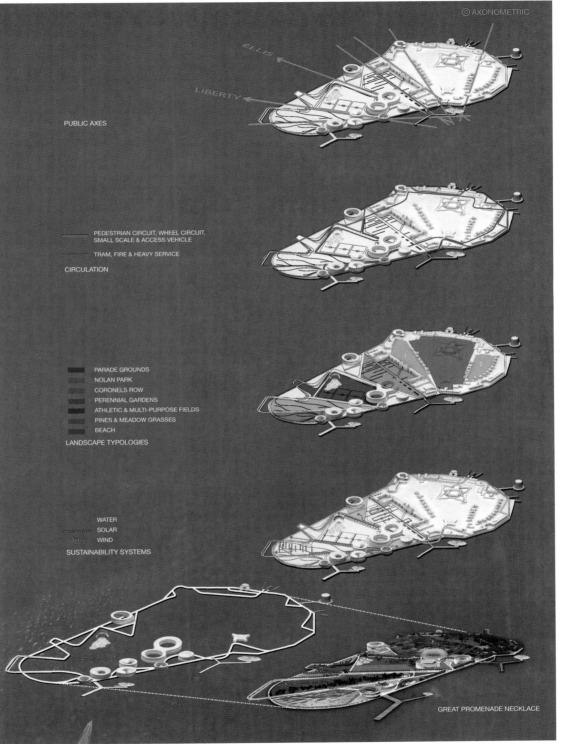

© AXONOMETRIC

PUBLIC AXES

PEDESTRIAN CIRCUIT, WHEEL CIRCUIT, SMALL SCALE & ACCESS VEHICLE

TRAM, FIRE & HEAVY SERVICE

CIRCULATION

PARADE GROUNDS
NOLAN PARK
CORONELS ROW
PERENNIAL GARDENS
ATHLETIC & MULTI-PURPOSE FIELDS
PINES & MEADOW GRASSES
BEACH

LANDSCAPE TYPOLOGIES

WATER
SOLAR
WIND

SUSTAINABILITY SYSTEMS

GREAT PROMENADE NECKLACE

03

01

02

03

04

05

Governor's Island was one of the first areas of Dutch settlement in the seventeenth century. The island, in the middle of New York Harbor, and 800 yards from Manhattan, became a strategic military fortification. The island was occupied and maintained by the United States Army and the United States Coast Guard through the twentieth century. The ninety-acre northern portion of the site is designated as a National Historic Landmark District. The competition brief called to maintain the northern art of the site as a historic district. New design is focused at the southern end to create 150 acres of new parkland.

The Hargreaves Associates team, which includes architect Michael Maltzan, sought to emphasize the contrasts of the Governor's Island site with the rest of the New York City Parks system. While most other New York City parks are enclaves within the city that emphasize interiority and escape from the hustle and bustle of the city, the design team saw that the park at Governor's Island has the opportunity to emphasize the view outwards to the city, inverting the typical New York City park experience. In order to privilege the exteriority of the site, the design features a Great Promenade Necklace, a continuous path that follows and expands the island's edge. A thickened

edge, the promenade is enriched with form and program. The promenade creates a circulation loop, facilitating all modes of movement around the island, from the leisurely stroller to the active runners, bikers and rollerbladers that zip through the entire city. A multi-circuit path, the promenade splits off to hover over the East River, engaging the water, widens at the shoreline to create an amphitheater, splits off to create trails through dunescapes, and spirals up to form architecture.

With the emphasis on viewshed, the team expanded the thickened edge at Public Axes – strategic locations that frame views to the Manhattan skyline, the Statue of Liberty, Ellis Island, the Verrazano Bridge, and Brooklyn. These nodes further serve to articulate the edge system and provide nodes that punctuate the flow of the promenade. Working inwards from the outer edge, the design team created zones of landscape typologies – dunes and beach, wetlands, pine barrens and oak drift – embedded with diverse program that create interior areas of exploration and rich experience once the fascination with the edge would fade. These typologies are juxtaposed without transition, echoing the program strategies of Plaza Park, Louisville Waterfront and Discovery Green in Houston.

01: The Great Promenade Necklace is a thickened edge enriched with form and program. 02: The Beach typology is embedded with diverse program. 03: The Pine Barrens ecological zone. 04: The design frames views the Statue of Liberty and other landmarks. 05: Vibrant gardens enrich the historic northern area.

01

02

03

Layered over the programmed zones is a calendar of programmed activities that further encourages a wide range of park visitors.

The phasing strategy of the project was designed to generate interest and community for the site over time. Without a residential community on the island to populate the park, the issue of generating interest in and getting people to the site is fundamental – would people come to the site at all? If there was a concert, would there be enough transportation to get people efficiently on and off the island? The Hargreaves Associates proposal emphasizes an approach that seeds

interests and activities on the site, creating a park constituency that would then demand the transportation infrastructure to support that community. A program oriented park, the scheme for Governor's Island responds to the particular conditions of New York, urban density and a diverse, active and creative population that seeks the fantastic, and mobilizes to enrich its own urban context.

04

05

06

01-03: Landscape typologies are juxtaposed without transition, including Wetland, Oak Drift, and Dunes. **04:** The view to the island from Manhattan. **05.06:** The park responds to urban density and a diverse, active and creative population that seeks the fantastic.

01

MAGOK WATERFRONT
Seoul, South Korea

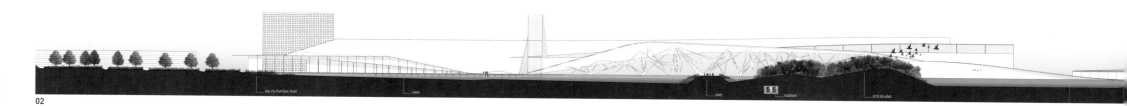

02

Magok Waterfront is an urban design project for a waterfront mixed-use urban development. This project is sited along the Han River in Seoul, South Korea. The open competition was organized by the city of Seoul, and Hargreaves Associates collaborated on the entry with the architecture firm officeDA. The design exploits the waterfront edge to facilitate both urban development engaged with the water, as well as the environmental development of ecological systems that saturate the site and enrich the human oriented buildings and programs. Physically, the design balances connections inward to urban Seoul with connections outward to the Han River and beyond. Experientially, the design creates deep connections to local ecologies, while the residential and commercial program remains physically separate from the environmental program. The western side of the site is oriented to the urban and mixed use development, creating an urban gateway on the waterfront. A series of pier typologies link the built structures with the extensions over the water, with piers and horizontal and vertical buildings interacting to create a variety of built forms integrated with landscape conditions.

01: Sited along the Han River in Seoul, this urban design project crafts a waterfront mixed-use urban development. **02:** Landscape, piers and architecture create a cohesive urban design.

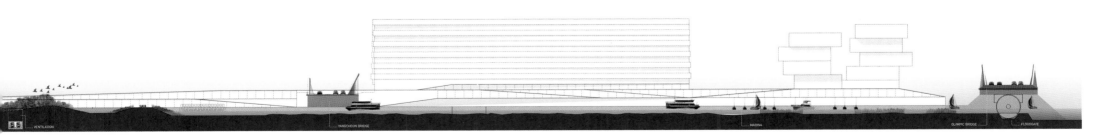

sectional matrix for mixed-use development

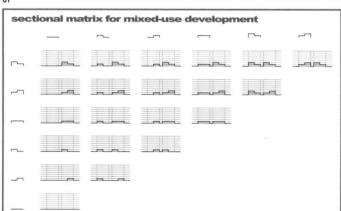

typical plinth

pedestrian
vehicular

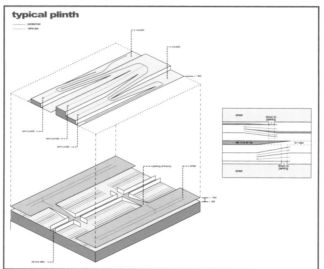

pier typologies
for development of residential finger piers

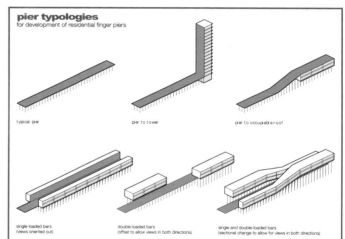

typical pier

pier to tower

pier to occupiable roof

single-loaded bars
(views oriented out)

double-loaded bars
(offset to allow views in both directions)

single and double-loaded bars
(sectional change to allow for views in both directions)

circulation

pedestrian
vehicular

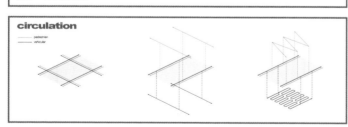

phasing plan for mixed-use plinth

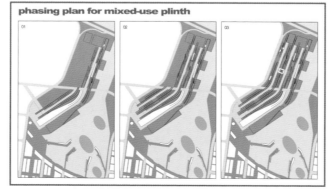

01   02   03

olympic highway bridge

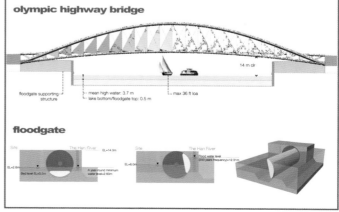

14 m clr

floodgate supporting
structure

mean high water: 3.7 m

max 36 ft loa

lake bottom/floodgate top: 0.5 m

floodgate

typical cross-section

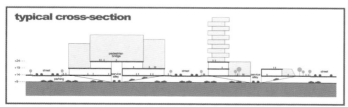

01

02

vehicular & pedestrian system

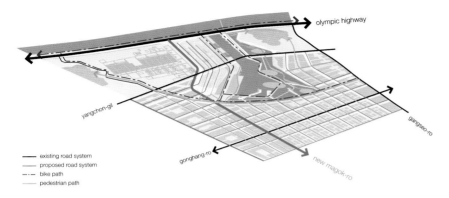

olympic highway

yangchon-gil

gangseo-ro

gonghang-ro

new magok-ro

— existing road system
— proposed road system
-·-·- bike path
— pedestrian path

transportation system

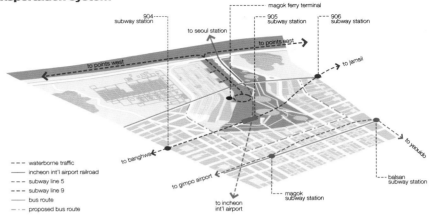

904 subway station
905 subway station
906 subway station
magok ferry terminal
to seoul station
to points east
to points west
to jamsil
to banghwa
to yeouido
to gimpo airport
balsan subway station
to incheon int'l airport
magok subway station

- - - waterborne traffic
— incheon int'l airport railroad
- - - subway line 5
- - - subway line 9
— bus route
-·-· proposed bus route

program

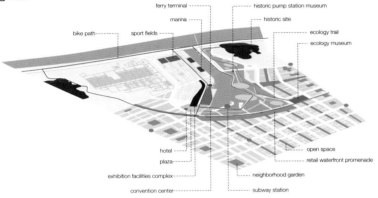

ferry terminal
marina
bike path
sport fields
hotel
plaza
exhibition facilities complex
convention center
historic pump station museum
historic site
ecology trail
ecology museum
open space
retail waterfront promenade
neighborhood garden
subway station

green system

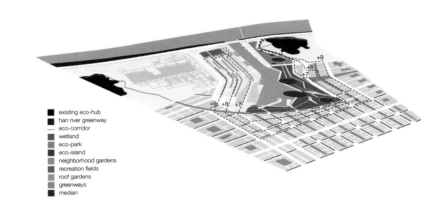

+9
+8
+7
+9
+8
+7

■ existing eco-hub
— han river greenway
— eco-corridor
■ wetland
■ eco-park
■ eco-island
■ neighborhood gardens
■ recreation fields
■ roof gardens
■ greenways
■ median

water management

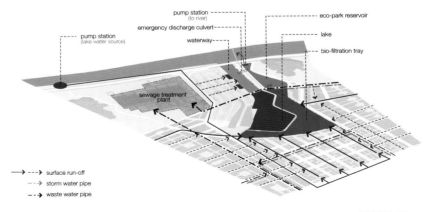

pump station (to river)
emergency discharge culvert
waterway
pump station (lake water source)
eco-park reservoir
lake
bio-filtration tray
sewage treatment plant

→ - - → surface run-off
- - → storm water pipe
- - → waste water pipe

Piers transition to towers in an L shape, shift up over buildings to create occupiable roofs, and have varied relationships to horizontal built structures to organize views out. On the eastern side of the site, the design creates a rich ecological buffer and creates systems to facilitate public access to the river and the intricate ecologies that thrive there.

01: Piers and vertical towers interact to create a variety of built forms integrated with the waterfront landscape.

The Han River flows through Seoul, dividing the city between North and South. The River flows west out of the city and toward the West Sea, connecting Seoul to its global context. The route across the Han was once a vital shipping route to China, now no longer used for shipping because of its border at its estuary with North Korea.

01

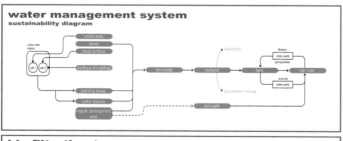

water management system
sustainability diagram

bio-filtration tray

ZONE 1_ 50~60cm : aquatic plants
ZONE 2_ 10~20cm: emergent plants
ZONE 3_ below 10cm : wet meadow

discharge pipe

01: The design creates an urban mixed use development that co-exists with a rich ecology.

east asia flyway

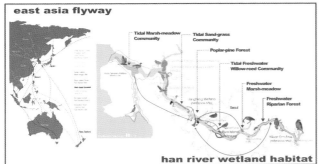

han river wetland habitat

eco island network

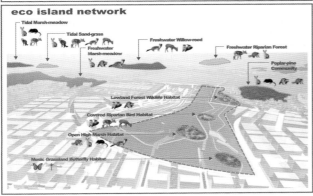

ecotype community variables

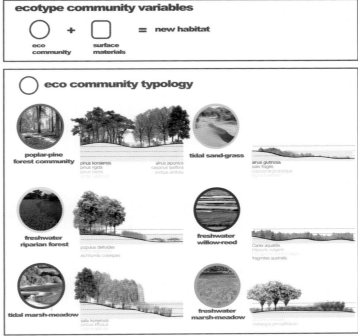

variety of habitats

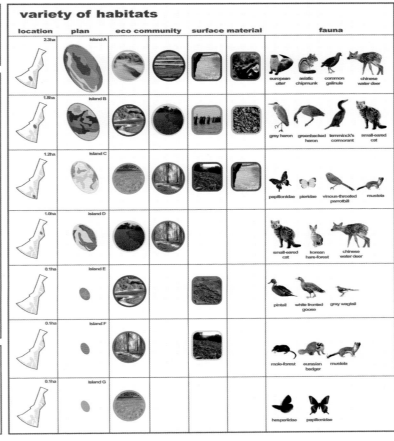

By connecting the Han River with urban Seoul, Hargreaves Associates' proposal seeks to renew these global relationships.

The design acts in multiple ways to enrich ecologies on site, enriching local ecological communities and supporting migrating species over the East Asia Flyway. As part of the development, the design creates habitat islands, terraced inlets, ecology boardwalks and trails through bio-filtration wetlands. Minimal but strategic interactions between people and the ecological systems are designed to highlight the ecologies without harming them. The habitat islands are set apart, with restricted access for people. While the animal habitat and people are kept in a balance, largely separated, the infrastructure of the two areas is integrated. A constructed wetland in the ecological area treats greywater from the developed portion of the site.

Urban connections are made back to Seoul through linkages of stormwater management infrastructure and public open spaces. These landscape spaces and functions weave the new urban development into the existing fabric of urban life. The design manipulates the topography of the urban edge to bring it closer to sea level, in order to create greater interactions with natural water systems, increasing the flow of stormwater and the effectiveness of the bioswale gardens.

01

02

03

01-03: Ecology and recreational uses exist side by side.

SOUTHWEST TENNESSEE
COMMUNITY COLLEGE

53B
53S

FEDERAL
PRISON

SHELBY
GOVERNMENT
OFFICES

CSX RAILROAD

53S (proposed extension)

MULLINS STATION ROAD

NEIGHBORHOOD PARK

HELIPAD

SPECIAL OPS

COUNTY JAIL

POLICE FACILITIES

SHELBY ROADS
DEPARTMENT

COMMUNITY ORCHARDS
BBQ PICNIC GARDENS
SENIOR GARDENS

SHOOTING
RANGE

ORNAMENTAL
GRASSES

TREE FARM

CHICKASAW
LAKE

PINE
LAKE

STABLES

SPORTS HOUSE

LUCIUS BURCH JR
NATURAL AREA

BISON
RANGE

CENTRAL
MEADOWS

RALEIGH LA GRANGE ROAD

BEAVER
LAKE

TERRACE
GARDENS

10' LOCK

LAKE HOUSE

WILDFLOWER
GARDENS

PATTERN
LAKE

DOG AREA

WOLF RIVER

RIVER HOUSE

PATRIOT
LAKE

FLOATING
POOL

SCHOOL
GARDENS

REGIONAL PARK

OVERFLOW
EVENT PARKING

HIKING TRAILS

WILLOW
LAKE

EVENT
AMPHITHEATER

MEANDER LAKES

DUCKS
UNLIMITED

MUMFORD BLVD

TREE HOUSE

CATCH 'EM LAKE

FARM HOUSE

34

GERMANTOWN PKWY

LUCIUS BURCH JR
NATURAL AREA

50B

EXISTING
LEVEE

10' LOCK

GREEN RV PARK
OVERFLOW PARKING

WOLF RIVER BLVD

LEVEE
PROMENADE

NATURE PARK

WOLF RIVER

PUMP HOUSE

AGRICULTURE PARK

01: Shelby Farms refigures an existing regional park in Memphis, Tennessee
with a new vast system of constructed lakes. **02:** The lakes create recreational
opportunities. **03:** An amphitheater creates a regional concert venue.

SHELBY FARMS PARK
Memphis, Tennessee

With the **Shelby Farms Park** competition entry, *Shelby Lakes Park*, Hargreaves Associates, working with architect Michael Maltzan, refigures an existing regional park in Memphis, Tennessee, creating a park for the 21st century. The massive regional park currently serves Memphis with 4500 acres of naturalized landscapes, trails and constructed lakes. The Hargreaves Associates strategy uses a new vast system of constructed lakes to dramatically refigure the park, creating a network of activities that builds on the existing site attractions. Embedded within the larger park, four smaller parks create focused nodes of activities. The Neighborhood Park borders the local neighborhoods and creates an intimately scaled park with playgrounds, picnic areas and gardens. The Regional 'World Class' Park offers amphitheater concert venues, water recreation and sports amenities. The Natural Park enhances the existing habitat oriented recreation of the facility and creates a unified experience of the natural systems of the park. The Agricultural Park synthesizes a productive landscape across the park. The existing agricultural research facilities are expanded upon with biofields and an additional research center. Within the park structure are *houses* – architecture designed by Michael Matzan that accommodates amenities, functioning as attractors throughout the park and supporting adjacent activities with equipment, parking and shuttle stops, restaurants and cafes. These nodes create markers in the landscape, viewed from the grounds, as well as places to climb and take in views of the entire park. This system of houses and parks creates a framework that organizes the extremely large park. These specialized parks create a rich experience for a variety of visitors.

The Wolf River flows along the southern border of the park. The new lake system would divert water at one end of the park at the Pump House and return it at the other, at the River House. The new lake system permeates the site, creating a park that can be completely navigated by boat, kayak or canoe. This new way of experiencing the site works in conjunction with a multivalent circulation system, providing dedicated circulation systems for joggers and walkers, horseback riders, cars, bicycles, etc.

02

03

01

02

03

01.02: A multivalent circulation system creates a distinct park experience facilitating confluences of park uses.

03: Site model.

Sequencing

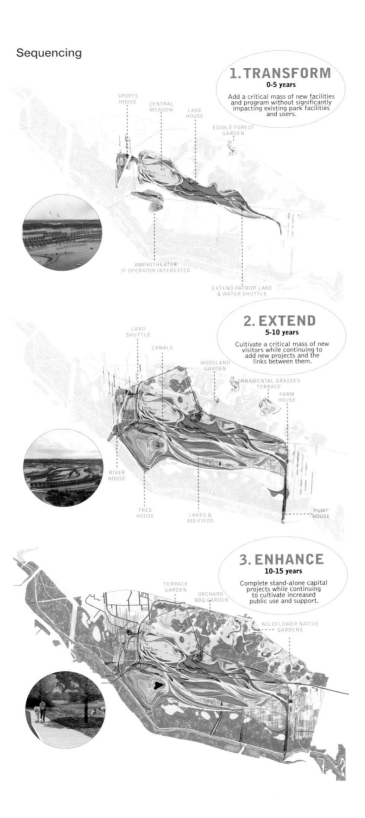

1. TRANSFORM
0-5 years
Add a critical mass of new facilities and program without significantly impacting existing park facilities and users.

SPORTS HOUSE
CENTRAL MEADOW
LAKE HOUSE
EDIBLE FOREST GARDEN
AMPHITHEATER IF OPERATOR INTERESTED
EXTEND PATRIOT LAKE & WATER SHUTTLE

2. EXTEND
5-10 years
Cultivate a critical mass of new visitors while continuing to add new projects and the links between them.

LAND SHUTTLE
CANALS
WOODLAND GARDEN
ORNAMENTAL GRASSES TERRACE
FARM HOUSE
RIVER HOUSE
TREE HOUSE
LAKES & BIO-FIELDS
PUMP HOUSE

3. ENHANCE
10-15 years
Complete stand-alone capital projects while continuing to cultivate increased public use and support.

TERRACE GARDEN
ORCHARD BBQ GARDEN
WILDFLOWER NATIVE GARDENS

This type of circulation, providing dedicated side-by-side paths creates a distinct park experience, facilitating a fantastic confluence. At any given moment the kayaker and horseback rider, for example, come together in an unusual heightened juxtaposition. This momentary circulation system also operates at the larger scale of the entire park, assisting conveyance across the 4500 acres. Hargreaves Associates designed a three-fold circulation system for navigating the extents of the site. There is a car loop for individual access, parking at each activity node within the park and two shuttle systems – one by land and one by water – that also navigate the park. The circulation system navigates nodes of recreational program that complement the existing uses of the park and are designed to update those uses and attract more people. The Lake House provides boat rentals and facilities for swimming. The Farm House accomodates the existing Agricenter International research facility. A new River Ecology Center continues the ecological outreach and environmental educating of the existing Shelby Farms.

Integrated within the park are sustainability systems, both for energy creation as well as financial sustainability. Energy creation is integrated within each park node. The *houses* have photovoltaic cells to trap solar energy and wind turbines that harness wind energy. The wind turbines are integrated into the tower structures and photovoltaics are placed on the roofs of the parking structures and shade structures. Hargreaves Associates designed opportunities for financial sustainability including restaurant operations, equipment rentals, amphitheaters that support performance events and plazas that host markets and festivals. Additionally, the facilities of the park can provide resources for regional job training. The Agricenter facilitates integration into local economies. A tree farm harvests trees from the site, provides jobs and creates a revenue stream for the park. The Shelby Farms Park proposal intensifies the uses of the existing park, amplifying them to create a sustainable park that is perceived through a landscape experience of the fantastic.

01

02

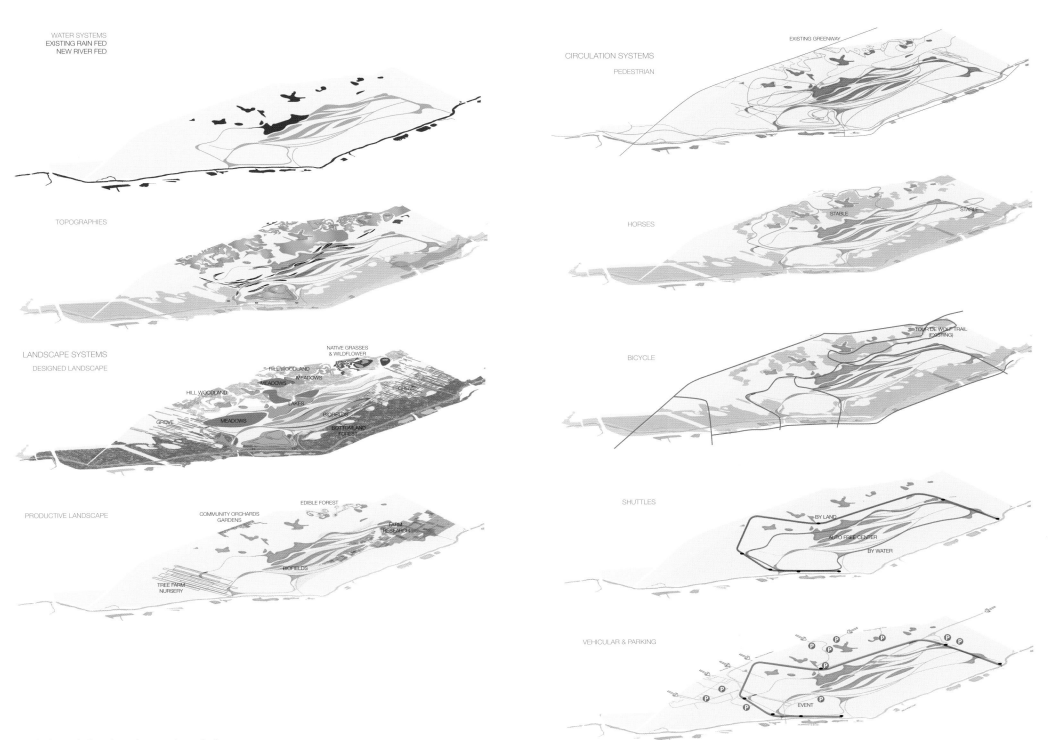

WATER SYSTEMS
EXISTING RAIN FED
NEW RIVER FED

CIRCULATION SYSTEMS

PEDESTRIAN

EXISTING GREENWAY

TOPOGRAPHIES

HORSES

STABLE   STABLE

LANDSCAPE SYSTEMS

DESIGNED LANDSCAPE

NATIVE GRASSES
& WILDFLOWER

HILL WOODLAND
MEADOWS
MEADOWS
HILL WOODLAND   GROVE
LAKES
GROVE   BIOFIELDS
MEADOWS   BOTTOMLAND
               FOREST

BICYCLE

TOUR DE WOLF TRAIL
(EXISTING)

PRODUCTIVE LANDSCAPE

EDIBLE FOREST

COMMUNITY ORCHARDS
GARDENS
                    FARM
                    RESEARCH

BIOFIELDS

TREE FARM
NURSERY

SHUTTLES

BY LAND

AUTO FREE CENTER

BY WATER

VEHICULAR & PARKING

EVENT

01: A productive park, the scheme incorporates agriculture.
02: The sustainable park incorporates native plant communities.

01

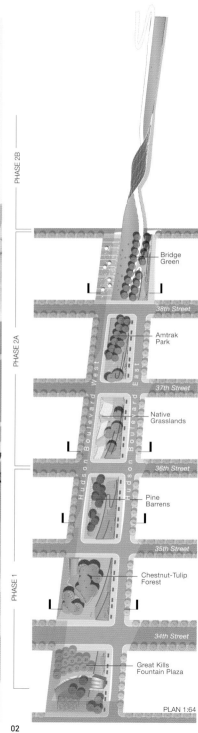

Bridge
Green

38th Street

Amtrak
Park

37th Street

Native
Grasslands

36th Street

Pine
Barrens

35th Street

Chestnut-Tulip
Forest

34th Street

Great Kills
Fountain Plaza

PLAN 1:64

PHASE 2B

PHASE 2A

PHASE 1

Hudson Boulevard West
Hudson Boulevard East

02

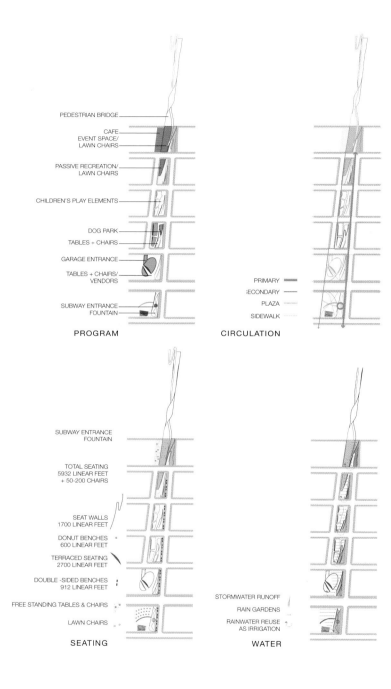

PEDESTRIAN BRIDGE

CAFE
EVENT SPACE/
LAWN CHAIRS

PASSIVE RECREATION/
LAWN CHAIRS

CHILDREN'S PLAY ELEMENTS

DOG PARK

TABLES + CHAIRS

GARAGE ENTRANCE

TABLES + CHAIRS/
VENDORS

SUBWAY ENTRANCE
FOUNTAIN

PROGRAM

PRIMARY
SECONDARY
PLAZA
SIDEWALK

CIRCULATION

SUBWAY ENTRANCE
FOUNTAIN

TOTAL SEATING
5932 LINEAR FEET
+ 50-200 CHAIRS

SEAT WALLS
1700 LINEAR FEET

DONUT BENCHES
600 LINEAR FEET

TERRACED SEATING
2700 LINEAR FEET

DOUBLE-SIDED BENCHES
912 LINEAR FEET

FREE STANDING TABLES & CHAIRS

LAWN CHAIRS

SEATING

STORMWATER RUNOFF

RAIN GARDENS

RAINWATER REUSE
AS IRRIGATION

WATER

01: *Episodic Archaeology* proposes a new mid block streetscape for the developing Hudson Yards neighborhood. **02**: The proposal re-situates lost ecosystems of pre-settlement Manhattan within the contemporary urban landscape. **03,04**: Mapping natural systems. **05,06**: At 34th Street, the Great Kills Fountain Plaza symbolically figures the water in the landscape as the subway entrance emerges.

HUDSON PARK AND BOULEVARD
New York, New York

In 2008 Hargreaves Associates participated in a competition for **Hudson Park and Boulevard**, a new mid-block streetscape for the developing Hudson Yards neighborhood on Manhattan's West Side. *Episodic Archaeology* posits an archaeological approach to the site, unearthing the lost ecosystems of pre-settlement Manhattan and resituating them within the contemporary urban landscape. The design proposal introduces pre-urban ecologies to a complex urban condition, saturated with the matter of urban infrastructure. Layered with program, Hargreaves Associates create a heightened atmosphere of unusual rich juxtapositions.

Reforming the lost ecosystems injects identity and meaning to the newly created residential district. The Chestnut Tulip Forest features the American Chestnut, once the hallmark of Eastern woodlands to urban Manhattan. The Chestnut was wiped out by a blight, but fungus resistant cultivars have been found and are being used to restore the tree to the environment. This zone also accommodates street vendors and weekend festivals. The Pitch Pine Barrens once stretched from Tribeca to Greenwich Village and across to Astor Place. At Hudson Boulevard, the Barrens are conceived of as a symbolic botanical collection, an excavation of pre-urban plant ecologies. A dog park and plaza space forms an additional layer to the space. The Hampstead Grasslands was once an extensive grassland ecosystem, covering 60,000 acres of the New York region. The short-grass prairie had established itself on glacier outwash and is considered a climax ecosystem. This ecotype provides habitat for several rare plant species, introducing native habitat to the new neighborhood. Children explore on large sculptural play objects here.

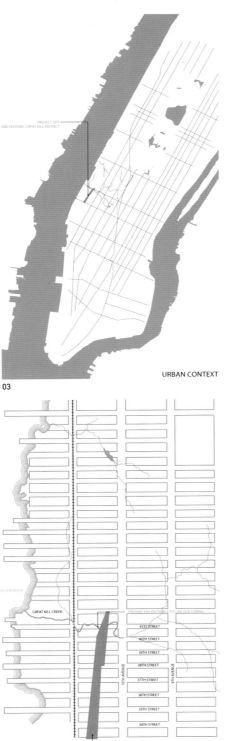

03

URBAN CONTEXT

04

GREAT KILL WATERSHED, 1788

05

06

LIGHTING AS SPECTACLE

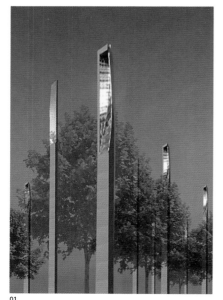

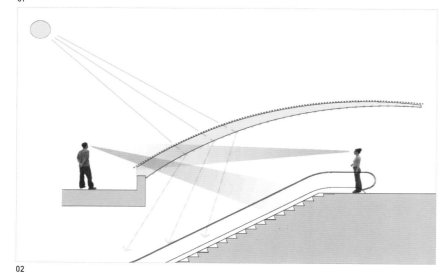

01

02

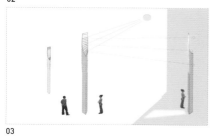

03

04

05

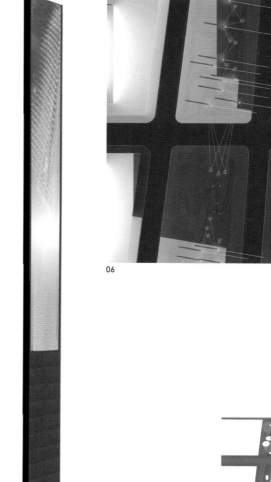

September 21 09:15 h

06

June 21 15:30 h

mast in direct sunlight
mast in shadow
sunlight
reflected light

07

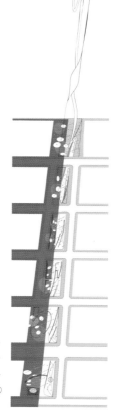

SUBWAY ENTRANCE
FOUNTAIN

LIGHT ELEMENT
REFLECTION PATTERN
LIGHT DIRECTION
REFLECTED DAYLIGHT

LIGHTING: DAY

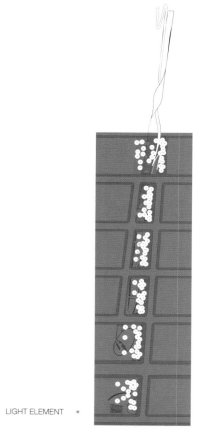

LIGHT ELEMENT

LIGHTING: NIGHT

Sustainable water infrastructure forms the substructure of the site, conceptually linked to the pre-urban hydrological system that once covered ten percent of Manhattan with wetlands. Stormwater runoff is channeled to a linear rain garden that stretches through the entire site, and the rainwater is re-purposed for on-site irrigation. At 34th Street, the Great Kills Fountain Plaza symbolically figures the water in the landscape. By introducing pre-settlement ecological zones to the contemporary urban condition, Hargreaves Associates unearth the palimpsest in a way that collapses and remakes time, figuring a complex understanding of public urban space. The new Boulevard acts as a journey of slippages, an experiential landscape of time, ecology and place.

Competitions allow Hargreaves Associates to address landscape architectural practice, to test ideas and to communicate with the field. In their competition entries, the firm explores multiple aspects of landscape architectural practice – phasing, urban design, process, the cultural park, ecology and sustainability. The ongoing exploration of these key ideas of landscape shape the work of the firm and the field as a whole. Hargreaves Associates' competition projects find new ways to express the design of landscape and further ways to deepen the public understanding and experience of landscape.

01-07: Light structures collect and produce light on the site.
08: Plan of the Chestnut Tulip Forest zone.

34TH/35TH STREET // CHESTNUT - TULIP FOREST

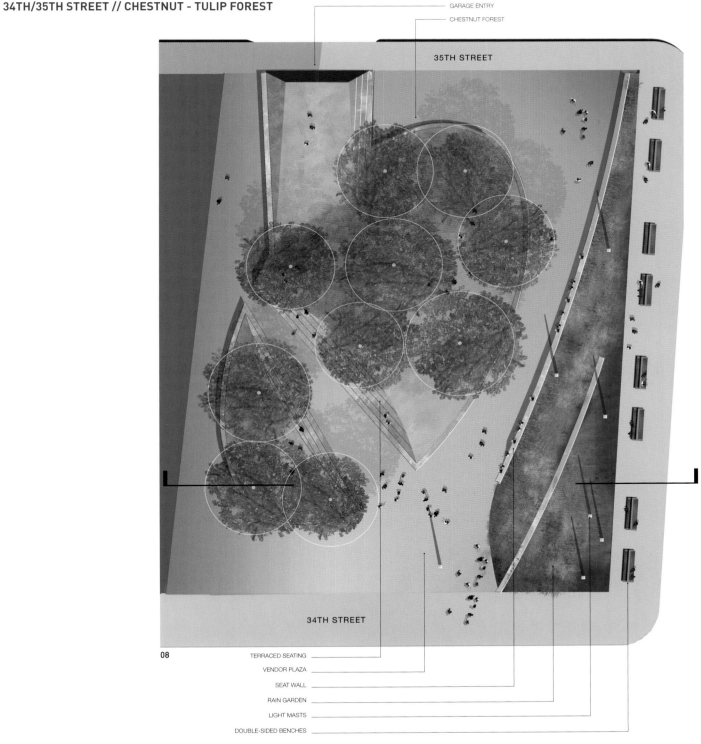

GARAGE ENTRY

CHESTNUT FOREST

35TH STREET

34TH STREET

08

TERRACED SEATING

VENDOR PLAZA

SEAT WALL

RAIN GARDEN

LIGHT MASTS

DOUBLE-SIDED BENCHES

01

02

PARKING GARAGE BELOW

PLAZA PATH — RAINGARDEN STORMWATER COLLECTION SYSTEM — 20" SIDEWALK — HUDSON BLVD EAST

03

35TH/36TH STREET // PINE BARRENS

04

01: The Chestnut Tulip Forest zone accommodates street vendors and weekend festivals. **02**: Resistant cultivars of the Chestnut are being used to restore the tree. **03**: Section. **04**: The Pitch Pine Barrens once stretched from Tribeca to Greenwich Village and across to Astor Place. **05**: Plan. **06**: Section.

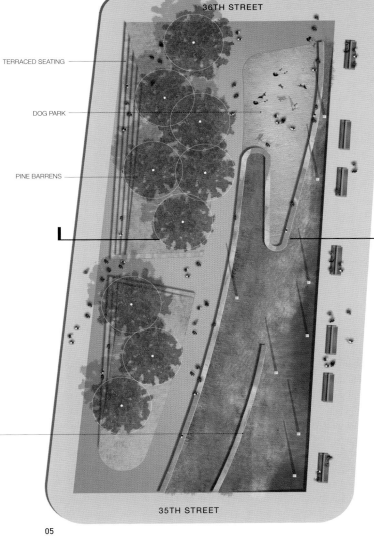

36TH STREET

TERRACED SEATING

DOG PARK

PINE BARRENS

RAIN GARDEN

35TH STREET

05

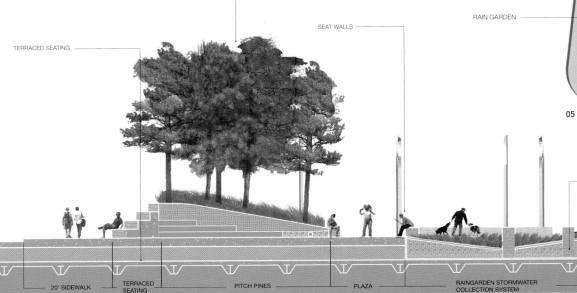

PITCH PINES

SEAT WALLS

TERRACED SEATING

RAINGARDEN STORMWATER
COLLECTION SYSTEM

1'
3'
9"

| 20' SIDEWALK | TERRACED SEATING | PITCH PINES | PLAZA | RAINGARDEN STORMWATER COLLECTION SYSTEM | 20' SIDEWALK | HUDSON BLVD EAST |

06

36TH/37TH STREET // HAMPSTEAD GRASSLANDS

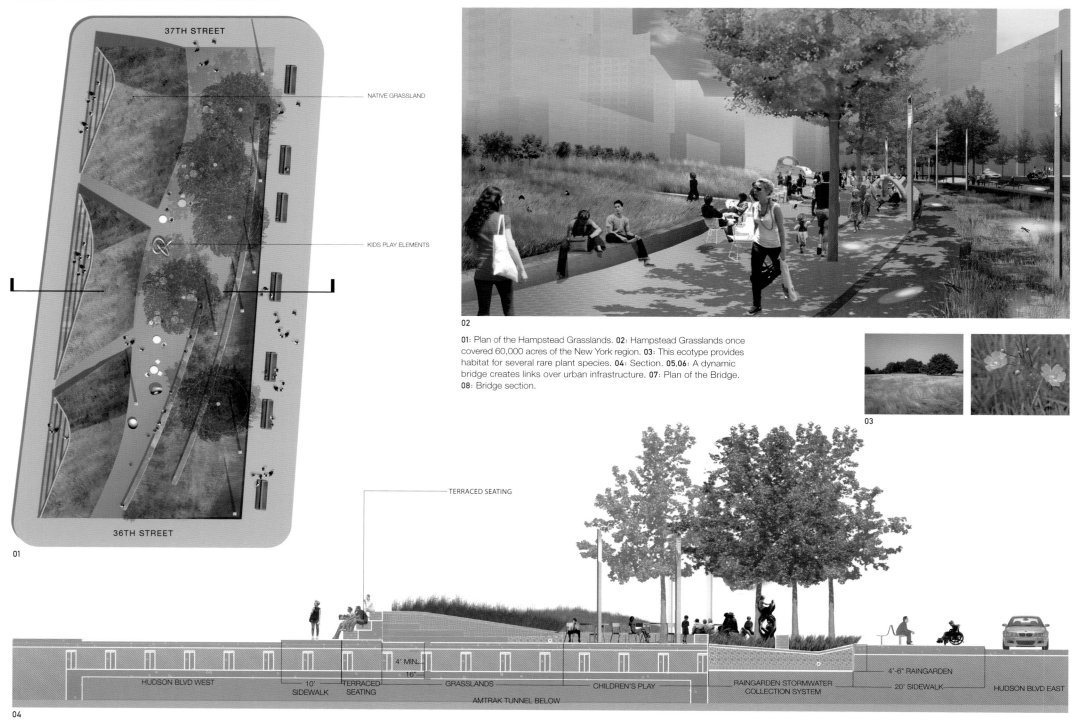

37TH STREET

NATIVE GRASSLAND

KIDS PLAY ELEMENTS

36TH STREET

01

02

01: Plan of the Hampstead Grasslands. 02: Hampstead Grasslands once covered 60,000 acres of the New York region. 03: This ecotype provides habitat for several rare plant species. 04: Section. 05,06: A dynamic bridge creates links over urban infrastructure. 07: Plan of the Bridge. 08: Bridge section.

03

TERRACED SEATING

HUDSON BLVD WEST   10'   TERRACED   GRASSLANDS   CHILDREN'S PLAY   RAINGARDEN STORMWATER   4'-6" RAINGARDEN
SIDEWALK   SEATING   COLLECTION SYSTEM   20' SIDEWALK   HUDSON BLVD EAST

4' MIN.

16"

AMTRAK TUNNEL BELOW

04

35TH/36TH STREET // BRIDGE GREEN

05

06

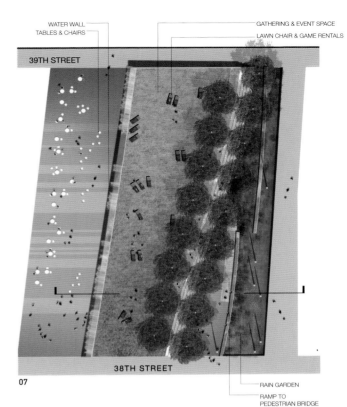

WATER WALL
TABLES & CHAIRS

GATHERING & EVENT SPACE
LAWN CHAIR & GAME RENTALS

39TH STREET

38TH STREET

RAIN GARDEN

RAMP TO
PEDESTRIAN BRIDGE

07

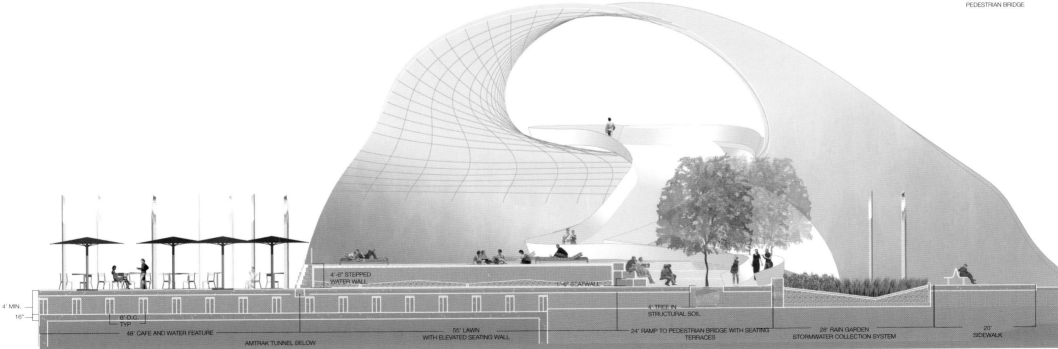

4'-6" STEPPED
WATER WALL

1'-6" SEATWALL

4' TREE IN
STRUCTURAL SOIL

4' MIN.

16"

6' O.C.
TYP

48' CAFE AND WATER FEATURE

AMTRAK TUNNEL BELOW

55' LAWN
WITH ELEVATED SEATING WALL

24' RAMP TO PEDESTRIAN BRIDGE WITH SEATING
TERRACES

28' RAIN GARDEN
STORMWATER COLLECTION SYSTEM

20'
SIDEWALK

08

A MAXIMAL PRACTICE

LIZ CAMPBELL KELLY

The look at the past twenty-five years of Hargreaves Associates encourages a look to the field of landscape architecture – the role the firm has played and how that role could evolve into the future.

After the prevailing adoption of post-war modernism and the environmental orthodoxy of the 1970s, landscape architects, led by a group of core practitioners, sought new ways to practice, a new formulation of what landscape could offer to culture as a whole.[1] Hargreaves Associates played a significant part in the crafting of a new body of landscape ideas, breaking new ground in the mid-1980s, and developing an engaged critical practice since that time. With a handful of other landscape architects, Hargreaves Associates have shown civic leaders, the public and other designers how landscape architecture can lead thinking around issues of the environment, infrastructure and urban development, solidifying a vital functional role for the profession in these areas. This engagement with usefulness does not limit the growth of the field in this particular direction, but rather gives landscape architects an expanded role in increasingly large projects and allows for more freedom to continually renew ideas of landscape place-making. A look at the past of Hargreaves Associates sheds light on the continuing development of landscape architecture as a profession, and suggests ways to anticipate and imagine the future.

Looking back
Looking at the role of the firm within the field, the remarkable achievement of Hargreaves Associates is twofold. The first chief accomplishment of the firm is, from their earliest projects, their break with the prevailing practice of an orthodox modernism in landscape architecture.[2] This, coupled with their ability to synthesize environmentalism into design, allowed the firm to create a new framework for the design and experience of landscape architecture. In his early essay "Post-Modernism Looks Beyond Itself," George Hargreaves describes the "failures" of modern landscape architecture as idealized, rigid constructions of space fixed to a stale diagram and symbolic relationship to site. Hargreaves opposed the increasingly formal qualities

of the modern landscapes that he summarized as "asymmetrically geometric and fluidly amorphous" both of which "revolve around an internal organization system, sharing with architecture and sculpture an idealized and invented space."[3] Also important to the critique of modernism, and insightful in the approach that the firm would take, is its lack of content. Hargreaves quotes art critic Kim Levin who describes the modernist sensibility: "It longed for perfection and demanded purity, clarity, order. And it denied everything else, especially the past."[4] For Hargreaves, modernist landscape architecture neglected both the history of the profession and the specificity of the site.

Hargreaves' use of the word *failure* is indicative of the role of the young firm within the profession. The young firm looks to the field, finds its foundations lacking, and then, in defiance, shows everyone a new way forward. The action of the *break* is what we seek from the young firm – to challenge the status quo and inject energy leading to the creation of new frameworks that define the field. The early built projects of the firm confronted the failures of the field head-on and succeeded in changing the language – in materials, sites and concepts – of landscape practice. By pursuing "open-endedness" – abandoning the internally organized compositions of modernism, embracing natural systems and phenomena, and working with the raw power of the large-scale sculptural site works – Hargreaves Associates created new methods and constructions of landscape architecture.[5] The work of the firm emphatically affirmed content in landscape experience and in extracted site histories. This defined a practice that, while appropriating some techniques and ways of thinking from the environmental artists, is germane to landscape architecture as a cultural practice. The emerging structure of the firm's designs created new ways for people to experience landscape architecture. The firm rethought and reformed the longstanding spatial typologies of park and plaza through integrated ideas of revealing large-scale natural phenomena and extractions of site histories. Hargreaves Associates' early projects were rebellious acts, injecting vital energy into the field. These projects transformed the way that

the profession is practiced, and created new ways for landscape architecture to be experienced.

Further, through the projects they choose to work on, and their attitudes to the potential of the site, Hargreaves Associates have consistently reformed our expectations of what the landscape can achieve. Early in their work, the firm showed a commitment to the brownfield site, remaking and transforming derelict sites into major public parks and nodes of green infrastructure as in *Byxbee Park*, *Parque do Tejo e Trancão*, *Crissy Field*, *Sydney Olympic 2000*, and *Chattanooga Renaissance Park*. Beyond the brownfield, Hargreaves Associates demonstrated new concepts in landscape architecture in projects like *Markings: Revelatory Landscapes* that explore the interrelationships of culture and ecology, and Candlestick Park that reconstitutes a dump site as a large-scale art informed earthwork as a public state park.

Another achievement of the firm is of duration – the development over twenty-five years of a coherent critical practice. As Corner writes in *Recovering Landscape*, "landscape architecture is not simply a reflection of culture but more an active instrument in the shaping of modern culture."[6] The critical practice of Hargreaves Associates is represented by a body of ideas manifested, reiterated, continually reinterpreted in built work. While the early projects broke new ground, their work since then has further explored the body of key concepts. The coherence of the themes of the firm's work – looking to the site, engaging the open-ended processes of ecologies and local histories – has emerged over their entire history of built work and critical essays. As the work of the firm has progressed, these themes and their manifestations in design strategies have evolved.

The Evolving Practice
A common thread through all Hargreaves Associates projects is site specificity. As the work of the firm developed over time, the approach to site specificity evolved and adapted to suit the particular project. Early projects explored a working methodology

of site specificity through repeated visits to the site to understand its potential. At *Candlestick Point* this prompted the large landform construction that organizes the entry sequence and interacts with the ephemeral experience of the wind on site. At *Byxbee Park* the design team looked to the site, again through repeated visits, to understand the landscape and find areas of prospect and points of attraction. This action of unlocking the potential of the site equates site specificity as the origin point of design. Each Hargreaves Associates project looks to the site to determine, at the most basic level, what the project is about. This kernel of content then manifests itself throughout all of the design content of the site, from overall spatial configuration to paving patterns. In this way, the work of Hargreaves Associates is not only site specific but also site-generated. This is seen most clearly at *Guadalupe River Park*, where a systematic set of conditions, working in concert with the Guadalupe River, generates the design of the park, which simultaneously functions as flood infrastructure, ecological corridor and recreational passage.

For Hargreaves Associates the concept of site-generated landscape architecture is as much rooted in the spatial structure of a place and its environmental phenomena as its historical and cultural narratives. In early work this is seen at *Plaza de César Chávez*, where the social and historical conditions of the site are manifested through the structure of the design and key

programmatic features – the fountain and festival plinths. *Crissy Field* also uses the past uses of the site as historic airfield to guide the structure and form of the park. Increasingly over time, as projects became more sophisticated in their construction and drew from layered design strategies, aspects of site specificity are integrated within the structural fabric of the park. This provides a strong foundation without site-specificity being the primary object of the design. The site construction of the *21st Century Waterfront* in Chattanooga and the *Clinton Presidential Center Park* function in this way, with site specificity forming an integral role but shared with other strategies. The *Los Angeles State Historic Park* maximizes the use of historic and cultural narratives of the site in the design of the park. In Los Angeles, this has a physical manifestation in the grain of the rail lines through the park, and is reinforced through interpretive displays. In this case, the history and culture of the site is brought to the forefront, through a diverse approach that lays out the overall structure of the park, the approach to plant material (agriculture and cultural), and the architectural structures at the park, which are structures that give information about the site history.

Spatial design strategies that were new and transformational in their early work take their place in a powerful toolkit of design strategies. For example, after incorporating sculptural landforms in early projects like *Candlestick Point* and *Byxbee Park* the firm

understands how landforms perform in the overall spatial construction of space, how they organize people and movement around them, how they are enjoyed by children and adults, and how they can opportunistically deal with problems on a site – the large mound at the *Sydney Olympics* contains and stabilizes the polluted fill from the site. As these functional criteria are understood, the earthworks exist not as art form but as a material of landscape architecture. For Hargreaves Associates, an earthwork can be deployed to create a number of known conditions. If a site has polluted fill, the earthwork becomes a known way that that a deficit can be turned into a strength. Landforms skillfully manipulate the movement of water on site to create functioning wetlands, while also screening the wastewater treatment facility at *Brightwater*. At *University Commons* at the University of Cincinnati, landforms provide identity for the campus while creating enclosure for the students. The firm also uses earthworks with different forms to create widely varied spatial relationships and sense of place. At *Parque do Tejo e Trancão* the earthworks express waste processes below ground. The large-scale sweeping landforms at *Candlestick Point* differ greatly from the playful serpentine mounds at *South Pointe Park*. As *Candlestick Point* uses landform to create the raw power of an unbridled nature, the landforms at *South Pointe Park* explore enjoyment while also providing access to ocean and bay views and the roof of the pavilion.

Another major evolution in the work of Hargreaves Associates is the treatment of program. While early projects explored ideas of process with little program to satisfy, later projects became larger in scope and with specific programmatic goals. Spatial design strategies for program emerged at *Plaza de César Chávez*, where program is linked to the narrative history of the site. The fountain at the crossroads of the park represents the intersection of the past – the artesian wells of the Guadalupe River – and the future, the hi-tech future of Silicon Valley. At *Louisville Waterfront Park*, Hargreaves Associates worked with the idea of linking program with landscape typology, and the juxtaposition of contrasting typology/program to produce heightened relationships between landscape types and interactions between different groups of people brought together at the park. The strategy of juxtaposition is also fundamental at *Crissy Field*, where the ecological program of the salt marsh abuts a wide range of recreation spaces. Hargreaves Associates produce meaning from these strategic juxtapositions, generating moments of landscape experience each time that aspect of the park is discovered by a visitor. In recent work, the strategy of juxtaposition has evolved into a strategy of layering. The most recent work of the firm aggressively explores issues of program. These works pursue flexible structures that allow for long-term adaptability and resilience of the built work and explore how people can engage with the design. At *Discovery Green* in Houston, Hargreaves Associates create a flexible and coherent structure that layers multiple programs across one space, maximizing the programmatic capabilities of the park.

With much of the discourse of the profession centered on the infrastructural scale, the projects of the firm that are the most often mentioned are the large-scale projects. Smaller projects, however, make up an important facet of the firm's overall practice. Site narrative, in *history*, *culture*, and *spatial volume*, is the focus of the firm's smaller projects. At *Plaza de César Chávez*, site history provided the basis for the layout and materials of the park. The firm looked to the site as the Spanish-formed town square

of San José, as well as the influences of the agricultural traditions of the area and its technological future in Silicon Valley. The synthesis of these aspects formed the structure of the site and provided the source for its features, including the surging fountain that references both the artesian wells of the site, which marked the territory for settlement, as well as its technological future. Cultural history also forms the origin for site narrative in such projects as the *Shaw Center for the Arts* in Baton Rouge. Here, the design is produced from the nearby Mississippi River, its river flows and the spatial movement of its barge traffic. The design is a unifying landscape for the arts center, which is an unusual hybrid of arts institutions in fine art and theater. At the *Museum of Emerging Science and Innovation* in Tokyo, the ancient cultural tradition of the Zen garden was transformed spatially with influences from the culture and forms of scientific exploration. The resulting landscape creates a design narrative that speaks directly to the function of the science museum within its cultural context. The *Minneapolis Residence* communicates its design narrative through spatial volume, choreographing the movement of spaces between architecture and landscape, and also as a sequence through landscape garden rooms that prompt movement from one to the next. The volumetric design of the landscape, in conjunction with the architecture and art collection, creates the site narrative – the interaction and interconnections of those elements. At *One Island East*, narrative is created through volumetric design coupled with intricate and specific details for seating, lighting and fountains. These site narratives of history, culture and spatial volume, executed precisely, create landscape experience in the firm's smaller projects.

With projects built at a spectrum of scales from small to large to infrastructural, the firm completes a full range of practice. The work of the firm at the *University of Cincinnati* is at both the large and small scale – from the campus-wide masterplan to the specific open spaces that the masterplan envisions. In a working relationship with the University of over fifteen years, Hargreaves Associates were able to shape the overall form of the campus

and see the reciprocal relationships between the masterplan and individual open spaces as the form of the overall campus emerged. The academic goals of the University evolved as projects were built and the masterplan was periodically revised to create the campus that would support those changing goals. Over the years of Hargreaves Associates' involvement on the project, the campus transformed from a car oriented commuter university to a twenty-four hour campus that emphasizes an active, vital student life. The project shows the relationship between scales of work, with long term and large scale strategic thinking reinforced with small projects.

Looking forward – a Maximal Practice
As we look to the young firm to reinvent ways of seeing and making, we look to the established firm to produce, develop and expand. The work of Hargreaves Associates over the next twenty-five years will surely continue to explore the core issues of both the profession at large and the specificity of the firm's critical practice – creating meaning through place-making while exploring environmental process, the culture of place and art. Hargreaves Associates' methods and modes of practice will be applied to the ever-shifting conversations of our larger culture. Currently these conversations are settling around issues of sustainability. Natural disasters associated with global warming, strife over the control of oil, and a recognition of the ongoing abuse of limited natural resources has prompted a sea change in attitudes towards sustainability and their relevance beyond the fringe and well into the mainstream. Where landscape architects have expertise in land management and understanding of how a range of technologies can work in conjunction with natural processes, other professionals such as engineers, architects, and "sustainability experts" are starting to tread, as sustainability becomes a more widespread goal, as well as another business opportunity.[7]

Hargreaves Associates have always incorporated groundbreaking sustainable technology within their work, without making this

overtly the mission. It is important for the firm not to relegate a project into the exclusive territory of science and the politics of the useful. Furthermore, the firm does not prioritize an environmental analysis over the cultural history of a place. An example of this is in their proposal entitled *New Orleans: The Big Fix* (not presented in this volume) where the firm devises a system of super levees that act as green infrastructure – providing elevated park and recreational spaces while protecting lowland New Orleans from the flooding of Lake Pontchartrain.[8] This proposal contrasts sharply with the many calls within the design community after Hurricane Katrina that suggest restoring this area to wetland. The firm found in their research for the project that the low-lying developed areas were occupied primarily by low income families. However, there was also a high percentage of home ownership, and these families wanted to return to their homes. This social factor led to the decision to create the super levees and system of green infrastructure rather that revert the area to wetland. For Hargreaves Associates, a commitment to sustainability cannot preclude the range of qualities that creates place-making. Landscape architecture has always served the classic oppositions of western culture – science and art, nature and culture, city and country – landscape architecture occupies these conflicting territories simultaneously and can use this ground to address sustainability within vibrant place-making.[9]

Hargreaves Associates occupy these opposing grounds through their strategy of juxtaposition and layering, creating a practice of the maximal. In this way, "usefulness" – whether manifested as sustainability or economic development – is embedded as a distinct layer of the project on separate but equal ground with other layers of history, culture, aesthetics, art, program and ecology. As landscape projects become more complex, this layering condenses multiple aspects into one place, creating meaning through the individual layers and their local interactions with other layers and as a whole. At *Guadalupe River Park*, distinct systems – the natural hydrological system, design interventions

to influence the hydrological system, and a recreational path system – create the total park. This strategy has been expanded upon in recent projects that create an integrated infrastructure that in turn supports multiple programs, optimizing flexibility and maximizing variety, as discussed earlier at *Discovery Green*. In that case, the park manages the range of program, uniting the experience of place with the support of the economic development goals of the city of Houston.[10]

In each project, Hargreaves Associates look for the performance potential of a landscape – what is the most that the landscape can do? These landscapes provide essential services for people that enrich quality of life. This is the practice of the *maximal*, developing landscapes whose structures incorporate utility and design elements. It is through this strategy that sustainability can be fully integrated with powerful landscape experience. Hargreaves Associates have worked on several large-scale green infrastructure projects that show the potential of large-scale sustainable landscapes. Projects like *Guadalupe River Park* and *Louisville Waterfront Park*, where the park surfaces are able to withstand massive flooding and protect the developed areas at higher elevations, are early examples of how landscape architecture can create sustainable urban infrastructure. At the *Sydney Olympics 2000*, the firm cleaned a brownfield site through the opportunity of the international event. At *Acuario Xochimilco* in Mexico City, the firm is currently integrating neighborhood waste infrastructure within the ecological and recreational structure of the overall park. The *London Olympics 2012 Park* is designed both for the Games and to transform into a permanent linear green infrastructure for East London. The *New Orleans: Reinventing the Crescent* project creates a continuous linear open space from an inaccessible industrial riverfront, with the goal of catalyzing development for the struggling city.

Hargreaves Associates incorporate green infrastructure while creating vibrant landscape experience. While their early work

that emphasizes open-ended process may seem to indicate a natural flow with the systems approach of the landscape urbanists, and Hargreaves Associates have indeed pursued a systems and operational approach to crafting landscape, the firm has always maintained the designer's hand in the design of the park, resisting the notion that ecological systems will take care of everything as the "tyrannies of ubiquitous process," a surrender not only of control, but of any intentionality of place making.[11] In the competition for the *Orange County Great Park,* an overall ecological framework is balanced with flexible phasing, dependent on the changing needs of the community as the park develops. This negotiation between process and design, science and art characterizes Hargreaves Associates' practice – work that engages process and natural systems while still asserting the hand of the designer. Hargreaves Associates hold fast to art, to the impulse and human desire to create and to make choices rather than leave things to chance. The firm seeks to reconcile open-ended process with intentionality.

The landscapes of Hargreaves Associates have a powerful character – vibrant places that are deeply embedded with functionality. This is both a result and a strategy, a clear intention at the outset of any project and an idea of what constitutes an engaging, potent landscape. These multivalent and layered works have resonance within distinct communities – the general public, and its many smaller user groups that enjoy the parks in a myriad of ways, and the planners, cities and private interests that look to the park to promote the growth and success of cities and regions. While there is a timeless aspect to the formulation of vital landscapes with functionality, as Olmsted's large parks clearly fit in to this model, for Hargreaves Associates the attention to these concepts has formed a specific practice of contemporary landscape architecture. The idea of landscape as animated designed space with embedded functionality has led the firm to create projects incorporating ever-increasing kinds of program, infrastructure and cultural meanings in new and subtle ways.

Within this model the firm inherently looks to the future. George Hargreaves describes the design techniques of the firm as systematic strategies to create *legibility*, *durability* and *longevity*, or put simply, "the things you do on the way to create projects that last generations."[12] The concepts of legibility, durability and longevity encompass a wide range of fundamental issues in landscape architecture, from the content in social, cultural and environmental aspects of projects, to new types of partnerships to build and maintain parks, to an increasingly global impact of today's practices. The firm is currently working on several large park projects that will leave a lasting impact

on their cities – the *London Olympics 2012* which after Games mode will anchor the revitalization of communities along the River Lea in East London, *Acuario Xochimilco* in Mexico City, *New Orleans: Reinventing the Crescent* and the *Los Angeles State Historic Park*, which activates a reengagement with the LA River in downtown. With an accrued knowledge of twenty-five years of practice and a continued dedication to dynamic place-making and bold form, the firm looks to the future to create vibrant landscape experience with an enduring impact on cities and regions.

BIBLIOGRAPHY

Project texts and Footnotes:
Chapter texts written by Liz Campbell Kelly based on interviews with George Hargreaves, Mary Margaret Jones, Glenn Allen, Gavin McMillan, Kirt Rieder, Catherine Miller, Ken Haines, Jacob Petersen, Megan Clark, Brian Jencek, Scott Smith, Alan Lewis, Andy Harris, Yoon Cho, James Smith, Matt Tucker, Tim Anderson, Lara Rose, Amy Seek and Rachel Laszlo.

Key Words and Phrases pp. 60-65
Anita Berrizbeitia

1. George Hargreaves, "Post Modernism Looks Beyond Itself" in *Landscape Architecture* (1983), pp. 60-65

2. George Hargreaves, "Large Parks: a Designer's Perspective" in *Large Parks*, Julia Czerniak and George Hargreaves, editors (New York, Princeton Architectural Press, 2007), pp. 121-173

3. Susan Rademacher, "Introduction: Toward Site Specificity" in *Hargreaves: Landscape Works*, Steve Hanson, editor (Tokyo, Process Architecture, Co., Ltd., 1996), p. 8.

4. George Hargreaves, "Most Influential Landscapes" in *Landscape Journal* (1993), p. 177; John Beardsley, "Poet of Landscape Process" in *Landscape Architecture* (December 1995)

5. George Hargreaves, "Post Modernism Looks Beyond Itself," p. 62.

6. George Hargreaves, "Post-Modernism Looks Beyond Itself," p. 61

7. George Hargreaves, "Point of View" in *Landscape Architecture* (1986), pp. 52-53, 110-112

Agency by Design pp. 164-169
Julia Czerniak

1. I would like to thank George Hargreaves and Liz Campbell Kelly for their thoughtful suggestions while developing this text.

For an insightful essay on landscape as an agent of urban regeneration, see Linda Pollak, "The Landscape of Urban Reclamation," in *Lotus International*, no. 128, 2006, pp.33–45. Pollak points out that "for a landscape to be an agent implies that it is not only present but also active and/or exerting power, rather than functioning as a passive backdrop for architecture and city." On the agency of landscape, see James Corner, "Ecology and Landscape as Agents of Creativity," in *Ecological Design and Planning*, eds. George Thompson and Frederick Steiner (New York: John Wiley & Sons, 1997), pp. 80–108. Alex Wall discusses a series of projects that target physical and cultural transformation by functioning as social and ecological agents: "They are instruments, or agents, for unfolding new urban realities, designed not so much for appearance and aesthetics as for their instigative and structuring potential." See "Programming the Urban Surface," in *Recovering Landscape: Essays in Contemporary Landscape Architecture*, ed. James Corner (New York: Princeton Architectural Press, 1999), pp. 232–249.

2. See Kevin Lynch, "The City Image and Its Elements," in *The Image of the City* (Cambridge, MA: MIT Press, 1960), pp. 91–118.

3. I refer here to the spatial qualities of Giovanni Battista Piranesi's fictitious etchings.

4. For a provocative look at the potentials of program, see Wall, "Programming the Urban Surface."

5. For more on the concept of resilience in parks, see "Legibility and Resilience," in *Large Parks*, ed. Julia Czerniak and George Hargreaves (New York: Princeton Architectural Press, 2007), pp. 214–251.

6. See Robert Venturi, "Contradictory Levels Continued: The Double-Functioning Element," in *Complexity and Contradiction in Architecture* (New York: Museum of Modern Art, 1966), p. 38.

7. Wall, "Programming the Urban Surface," p. 245.

8. In conversations with Hargreaves' Senior Principal and President Mary Margaret Jones regarding her work at the American Academy in Rome.

9. Hargreaves Associates project descriptions.

10. See my introduction, "Appearance and Performance:

Landscape at Downsview," in *CASE: Downsview Park Toronto* (New York: Prestel and the Harvard University Graduate School of Design, 2001), pp. 12–23.

11. For more on the relationship of site to Hargreaves' work, see "Looking Back at Landscape Urbanism: Speculations on Site," in *The Landscape Urbanism Reader*, ed. Charles Waldheim (New York: Princeton Architectural Press, 2006).

12. In "The Word Itself," *Discovering the Vernacular Landscape* (New Haven: Yale University Press, 1984), 8, cultural geographer J.B. Jackson writes "A landscape is thus a space deliberately created to speed-up or slow-down the process of nature." He further states that this "represents man taking upon himself the role of time." Thanks to Jacob Brown for reminding me of this reference.

13. For an early interview with George Hargreaves that is still surprisingly pertinent to their practice, see "Point of View," in *Landscape Architecture Magazine*, November/ December 1986, pp. 52–53, 110–112.

14. This definition is from the Regional Ecosystem Office's (REO) *Information Center Definitions*, retrieved on March 3, 2009, http://www.reo.gov/general/definitions.

15. Thanks to Jacob Petersen, Principal at Hargreaves Associates, for explaining the park's sustainable strategies.

16. See George Hargreaves and Liz Campbell Kelly's thoughtful essay on water infrastructure, "Interventions in Hydrology," in *Water: Design and Management*, Topos 59, 2007, pp. 50–57.

17. Combined sewer overflows (CSOs) are commonplace events in cities with aging infrastructure, in which the system that collects sewage is connected to the one that collects storm-water, and during a storm event regularly releases untreated sewage into water bodies.

18. Green infrastructure is commonly understood as an interconnected network of open spaces that naturally manages storm-water, reduces flooding risk, and improves water quality.

19. Thanks to Gavin McMillan, Principal of Hargreaves Associates, for pointing this out.

20. See *Economic Report: the Impact of Louisville's Waterfront Park*, Fall 2007, published on http://

www.louisvillewaterfront.com/documents/Economic_ Impact_2007.pdf

21. Ibid.

22. See *21st Century Waterfront Plan Fulfills Chattanooga's 20-Year Vision*, published on http://www.chattanoogacando. org/newsandvideo/.

23. My knowledge of this project is formed largely through drawings supplied by Hargreaves Associates, the press release from the Olympic Delivery Authority from November 6, 2008, and conversations with George Hargreaves.

24. George Hargreaves, as quoted in "London 2012 Unveils a New Type of Park for the 21st Century," November 6, 2008, press release supplied by the designer.

25. Ibid.

Competitions pp. 238-285

1. Julia Czerniak and George Hargreaves, ed. *Large Parks*, Princeton Architectural Press, New York, 2007.

Landscape Experience: A Maximal Practice pp. 286-291

1. In *Recovering Landscape* James Corner cites the "remarkable resurgence of interest in landscape topics" of the 90's and describes Hargreaves Associates as contributing to the re-engaged practice, who he says "bridge(s) the gap between artistic expression and ecological technique." *Recovering Landscape*, editor James Corner, (Princeton Architectural Press, New York, 1999), p. 18.

2. For a more complete description of modernism in landscape architecture, see Marc Treib, "Axioms for a Modern Landscape Architecture," in *Modern Landscape Architecture: a Critical Review*, (the MIT Press, Cambrige MA, 1989), pp. 47-53.

3. George Hargreaves, "Post Modernism Looks Beyond Itself." *Landscape Achitecture*, p. 60.

4. Ibid, p. 60.

5. Anita Berrizbeitia discusses this in further detail in Key Words and Phrases, pp. 60-65.

6. James Corner, "Recovering Landscape as a Critical Cultural Practice" in *Recovering Landscape*, ed. James Corner (Princeton Architectural Press, New York, 1999), p. 1.

7. Thanks to Claire Fellman for an engaging conversation about sustainability – the opportunities for landscape architecture, New York, April 2009.

8. *Symposium Newer Orleans* held by Nirov, the Netherlands Institute for Planning and Housing, March 2006. Exhibition at the Netherlands Architecture Institute, Rotterdam January 20- March 12, 2006.

9. Raymond Williams, *Keywords: A Vocabulary of Culture and Society*, (Oxford University Press, 1985). See definitions for *city*, *country*, *art*, *science*, *nature* and *culture*.

10. Julia Czerniak further discusses how landscape architecture catalyzes urban development in "Agency By Design," pp. 164-169.

11. George Hargreaves, "Large Parks: A Designer's Perspective" in *Large Parks*, ed. Julia Czerniak and George Hargreaves, (Princeton Architectural Press, 2007), p. 171.

12. Telephone interview with George Hargreaves, New York/ London, April 2009.

PHOTOGRAPHY CREDITS

John Gollings Photography
Front and back cover. *Byxbee Park* 10/11; 16; 17, images 01, 04, 05. *Louisville Waterfront Park* 22/23; 25-27; 30; 31. *Crissy Field* 42, image 01. *21st Century Waterfront* 44; 45; 46 image 01 and 02; 51, image 02. "Key Words and Phrases" 61, fig. 1 (Byxbee Park). *University of Cincinnati* 66/67; 69; 71; 73, image 02; 74-77; 78, image 01; 80/81; 83; 84, image 02; 85; 86, image 01; 87, image 04; 88; 89; 90, image 01; 91, image 04; 92, image 02; 93; 94; 95, image 03. *Sydney Olympics 2000* 7; 98-108; 109, images 03, 05. *William J. Clinton Presidential Center Park* 112-120; 121, image 02; 122-123. *One Island East* 156-163. "Agency by Design" 164, fig. 4; 165, fig 6, 7. *Discovery Green* 170/171; 172-174; 175, image 02, 03; 176/177, top row, second, third and fourth images, middle row third image, bottom row fifth image; 178; 179; 181. *Chattanooga Renaissance Park* 206-208; 210-211. "A Maximal Practice" 289 (*Discovery Green*).

Geoffrey Carr Photography
Louisville Waterfront Park 28

David Sanger
Crissy Field 34 image 02; 36; 37; 38; 43, image 03, 04

Robert Campbell
Crissy Field 35

Dan Euser Waterarchitecture
21st Century Waterfront 51, image 03

University of Cincinnati Office of the University Architect
University of Cincinnati 79, image 03

University of Cincinnati / Jay Yocis
University of Cincinnati 97, image 03

glaserworks
University of Cincinnati 92, image 01

Alan Karchmer / Esto
University of Cincinnati 92, image 03; 95, image 02; 96; 97, image 02

Timothy Hursley
William J. Clinton Presidential Center Park 111
Shaw Center for the Arts 149

Richard Barnes
Markings- Revelatory Landscapes 126

Soundview Aerial Photography
Brightwater Mitigation Area 129, image 04

Don Wong
Minneapolis Residence 134, image 01; 135, 136, image 01; 139, image 03

Hirokazu Yokose / SS Tokyo
National Museum of Emerging Science and Innovation 2; 140-145

Julia Czerniak
"Agency by Design" 164 fig. 1 (*Shaw Center for the Arts*); 165, fig 5 (*Louisville Waterfront Park*)

Robert Foster, GroundEscape LLC
South Pointe Park 190; 195; 196, top row left; 197, middle row; 198; 201, middle row, middle. "A Maximal Practice" 291

Barry Miller, Savino Miller Design Studio
South Pointe Park 196, middle row, middle; 199; 200, bottom row, right

Amanda Cox
South Pointe Park 200, middle row, middle; 201, bottom row, right

Lauren Griffith
Discovery Green 176/177, bottom row, first, second, fourth image

Rod Evans, Sherwood Construction Co
American Indian Cultural Center 296/297

Centennial Builders, joint venture of Manhattan Construction and Flintco Construction
American Indian Cultural Center 294/295; 298/299

All other images courtesy of Hargreaves Associates, including photographs by staff:

Villa Zapu, Candlestick Park
Glenn Allen

Plaza de César Chávez, Byxbee Park, Guadalupe River Park, Guadalupe Gardens
Mary Margaret Jones, Glenn Allen

Louisville Waterfront Park
Glenn Allen, Steve Hanson

Parque do Tejo e Trancão, Sydney Olympics 2000
Mary Margaret Jones

Crissy Field
George Hargreaves, Mary Margaret Jones, Kirt Rieder, Lara Rose

21st Century Waterfront
Gavin McMillan, Anna Horner

University of Cincinnati
George Hargreaves, Mary Margaret Jones, Glenn Allen, Kirt Rieder, Marcel Wilson, Steve Hanson

Markings: Revelatory Landscapes
Marcel Wilson

Brightwater Mitigation Area, Minneapolis Residence
Lara Rose

Shaw Center for the Arts
George Hargreaves, Kirt Rieder, Alan Lewis

South Pointe Park
George Hargreaves, Gavin McMillan, Matt Tucker

Discovery Green
Lara Rose, Jacob Petersen

PROJECT CREDITS

EARLY DAYS

Project: Villa Zapu
Location: Napa, California
Client: Private
Dates: 1985-1986
Size: 120 acres
Architect: David Connor Design

Project: Plaza de César Chávez / Plaza Park
Location: San José, California
Client: San José Redevelopment Agency
Dates: 1986-1989
Size: 2.5 acres
Fountain Engineer: Fountain Tech

Project: Candlestick Point State
Recreation Area
Location: San Francisco, California
Client: State of California Parks and Recreation
Dates: 1985-1987
Size: 18 acres
Architect: MACK architect(s)
Artist: Doug Hollis

Project: Byxbee Park
Location: Palo Alto, California
Client: City of Palo Alto
Dates: 1988-1990

Size: 150 acre master plan /
35 acres phase 1 construction
Artist: Peter Richards, Michael Oppenheimer
Architect: Davis Davis Architects

Project: Guadalupe River Park
Location: San José, California
Client: San José Redevelopment Agency,
Santa Clara Valley Water District,
US Army Corps of Engineers
Dates: 1988-1999
Size: three miles
Civil and Hydrological Engineer:
AN West, Inc
Geotechnical Engineer: AGS, Inc.
Ecological and Environmental Planning:
H.T. Harvey and Associates

Project: Guadalupe Gardens
Location: San José, California
Client: Recreation Parks &
Community Service
Dates: 1988-1990
Size: 4 acres

Project: Guadalupe Confluence Point
Location: San José, California
Client: San José Redevelopment Agency

Dates: 1992-1996
Size: 1.5 acres
Architect: jones, partners: architecture

CULTURES AND WATER

Project: Louisville Waterfront Park
Location: Louisville, Kentucky
Client: Waterfront Development Corporation
Dates: Master Plan: 1990 – 1996;
Phase 1: 1994 – 1999;
Phase 2: 2000 – 2004;
Phase 3: 2005– 2009
Size: Master Plan: 120 acres;
Phase 1: 52 acres; Phase 2: 20 acres;
Phase 3: 13 acres
Architect: Bravura Corporation
Fountain Engineer: Dan Euser
Waterarchitecture

Project: Parque do Tejo e Trancão
Location: Lisbon, Portugal
Client: Parque Expo 98
Dates: 1994 - 1998
Size: 160 acres
Associate Landscape Architect: PROAP

Project: Crissy Field
Location: San Francisco, California

Client: Golden Gate National Parks Association
Dates: 1994 - 2001
Size: 100 acres
Wetland Hydrologic Design: Philip Williams &
Associates
Civil Engineer: Moffatt & Nichol Engineers
Habitat Biologist: Wetland Research Associates
Architect: Tanner Leddy Maytum Stacy

Project: 21st Century Waterfront
Location: Chattanooga, Tennessee
Client: RiverCity Company
Dates: 2002-2005
Size: Master Plan: 129 acres Phase 1: 63 acres
Associate Architect (master plan phase):
Schwartz/Silver Architects
Artists: James Carpenter, Gadugi Team
Fountain Engineer: Dan Euser
Waterarchitecture

Project: New Orleans Waterfront:
Reinventing the Crescent
Location: New Orleans, Louisiana
Client: New Orleans Building Corporation
Dates: 2007 – 2008, Phase 1 2008-present
Size: six linear miles
Architect: TEN Arquitectos,
Eskew+Dumez+Ripple, Chan Krieger Sieniewicz

Project: Mission Rock (Sea Wall Lot 337)
Location: San Francisco, California
Client: Wilson Meany Sullivan
Farallon Capital Management, L.L.C.
San Francisco Giants
Kenwood Investments
Stockbridge Capital
The Cordish Company
Dates: 2008-2009
Size: 16 acres
Architect: Perkins+Will,
Beyer Blinder Belle Architects
& Planners

UNCOMMON PLACES
Project: University of Cincinnati Master Plan,
Master Plan Update I, Master Plan 2000
Location: Cincinnati, Ohio
Client: University of Cincinnati
Dates: 1989- 2000
Size: 200 acres

Project: Aronoff Center for Design
Location: Cincinnati, Ohio
Client: University of Cincinnati
Dates: 1993-1996
Size: 2.9 acres
Architect: Eisenman Architects

Project: Library Square
Location: Cincinnati, Ohio
Client: University of Cincinnati
Dates: 1995-1998
Size: 1 acre
Engineering Research Center Architect:
Michael Graves & Associates
Stairway Connector Architect: jones, partners:
architecture

Project: University Commons
Location: Cincinnati, Ohio
Client: University of Cincinnati
Dates: 1995-2000
Size: 3.2 acres
Architect: Frank O. Gehry and Associates
Artists: Joel Shapiro, George Rickey, Terry Allen

Project: Campus Green
Location: Cincinnati, Ohio
Client: University of Cincinnati
Dates: 1997-2000
Size: 2.7 acres
Fountain Engineer: Dan Euser
Waterarchitecture

Project: Sigma Sigma Commons
Location: Cincinnati, Ohio

Client: University of Cincinnati
Dates: 1995-1998
Size: 3.4 acres
Tower Architect: Machado and Silvetti
Associates

Project: University Plaza
Location: Cincinnati, Ohio
Client: University of Cincinnati
Dates: 2000-2002
Size: 32,628 sf
Architect: Leers Weinzapfel Associates
Architects
Associate Architect: GBBN architects
Fountain Engineer: Dan Euser
Waterarchitecture

Project: Zimmer Plaza
Location: Cincinnati, Ohio
Client: University of Cincinnati
Dates: 1999-2006
Size: 34,000 sf
Artist: Kenneth Snelson

Project: Main Street
Location: Cincinnati, Ohio
Client: University of Cincinnati
Dates: 2000-2005

Size: 8.48 acres
Architect: Gwathmey Siegel & Associates
Architects, Moore Ruble Yudell Architects &
Planners, Morphosis
Associate Architects: Glaserworks, KZF
Design, GBBN architects

Project: Sydney Olympics 2000
Location: Sydney, Australia
Client: Olympic Coordination Authority
Dates: 1996-2000
Size: Masteplan: 1900 acres /
Plaza and Water
Features: 31.5 acres
Associate Landscape Architects:
The Government Architect Design Directorate
(GADD), Schaffer Barnsley, Anton James,
Gavin McMillan
Architect: Tonkin Zulaikha Greer
Fountain Engineer: Sydney Fountains
Waterforms

IMAGES ON PAGES 194-199: American Indian Cultural
Center, Oklahoma City, OK.

PROJECT CREDITS

Project: William J. Clinton Presidential
Center Park
Location: Little Rock, Arkansas
Client: William J. Clinton Foundation
Dates: 2000-2005
Size: 30 acres
Architect: Polshek Partnership Architects
Associate Landscape Architect: Landscape
Architecture Incorporated
Fountain Engineer: Dan Euser
Waterarchitecture

Project: Markings- Revelatory Landscapes
Location: San José, California
Client: Curator Aaron Betsky, SFMOMA
Dates: 2001
Size: 4 acres
Poet: Julian Lang

Project: Brightwater Mitigation Area
Location: Snohomish County, Washington
Client: King County
Dates: 2002-
Size: Northern Mitigation Area 40 acres
Entire Site: 110 acres
Engineer: CH2M Hill and Brown&Caldwell
Salmon Habitat: Daley Design
Environmental Consulting: 2020 Engineering

Education & Interpretive Systems:
Lehrman Cameron Studio
Artists: Jann Rosen-Queralt, Buster Simpson
and Ellen Sollod

SMALLER
Project: Minneapolis Residence
Location: Minneapolis, Minnesota
Client: Private
Dates: 1996-1997
Size: withheld
Architect: Vincent James Associate Architects
Artist: James Carpenter

Project: National Museum of Emerging Science
and Innovation
Location: Tokyo, Japan
Client: Japan Science and Technology Agency
Dates: 1999-2001
Size: 12.36 acres
Architect: Nikken Sekkei Ltd

Project: Belo Gardens
Location: Dallas, Texas
Client: Belo Corp and Dallas Park
and Recreation Department
Dates: 2006-
Size: 1.5 acres

Associate Landscape Architect:
Carter & Burgess

Project: Shaw Center for the Arts
Location: Baton Rouge, Louisiana
Client: The Baton Rouge Area
Foundation / State of Louisiana /
Louisiana State University Museum
of Art / Louisiana State University
School of Art / Louisiana State University
Laboratory of Creative Arts & Technology /
Louisiana State University Foundation /
City of Baton Rouge, Parish of East
Baton Rouge
Dates: 2002-2005
Size: 3.8 acres
Architect: Schwartz/Silver Architects,
and Eskew+Dumez+Ripple

Project: One Island East
Location: Hong Kong, China
Client: Swire Properties Limited
Dates: 2006-2008
Size: 9.5 acres
Architect: Wong & Ouyang HK Ltd.
Lighting: L'Observatoire International NYC
Fountain Engineer:
P&A Engineering, HK

URBAN PARKS
Project: Discovery Green
Location: Houston, Texas
Client: Discovery Green Conservancy
Dates: 2005-2008
Size: 12 acres
Architect: PageSoutherlandPage
Artists: Doug Hollis, Margo Sawyer
Associate Landscape Architect:
Lauren Griffith Associates
Fountain Engineer: Dan Euser
Waterarchitecture

Project: South Waterfront Neighborhood Park
Location: Portland, Oregon
Client: Portland Parks & Recreation/
Portland Development Commission
Dates: 2008-2009
Size: 2 acres
Artist: Doug Hollis
Associate Landscape Architect: Lango
Hansen Landscape Architects
Fountain Engineer:
Dan Euser Waterarchitecture

Project: South Pointe Park
Location: Miami Beach, Florida
Client: City of Miami Beach Capital

Improvement Projects
Dates: 2005-2009
Size: 19.3 acres
Architect: William Lane Architects
Associate Landscape Architect:
Savino Miller Design Studio

Project: Project: Acuario Xochimilco
Location: Mexico City, Mexico
Client: Gobierno DF - Fideicomiso
Complejo Ambiental Xochimilco
Dates: 2007-
Size: 1300 acres
Architect: TEN Arquitectos
Environmental, Structural,
Transportation Engineer: Arup

Project: Renaissance Park
Location: Chattanooga, Tennessee
Client: RiverCity Company
Dates: 2003-2005
Size: 23 acres
Architect: Eskew+Dumez+Ripple

Project: Los Angeles State Historic Park
Location: Los Angeles, California
Client: California State Parks
Dates: 2006-

Size: 32 acres
Architect: Michael Maltzan Architecture
Interpretive Planner: Ralph Appelbaum
Associates
Associate Landscape Architect: Katherine
Spitz Associates
Associate Urban Design: Arthur Golding

Project: London 2012 Olympics
Location: London, United Kingdom
Client: Olympic Delivery Authority
Dates: 2008-
Size: 252 acres
Executive Landscape Architect: LDA Design

COMPETITIONS
Project: Orange County Great Park
Location: Los Angeles, California
Client: Orange County Great Park Corporation
Dates: 2005
Size: 3700 acres
Architect: Morphosis

Project: East Darling Harbour
Location: Sydney Australia
Client: Government of New South Wales
Dates: 2005-2006
Size: 54 acres

Architect: Morphosis
Associate Architects: Project Architecture

Project: Los Angeles State Historic Park
Location: Los Angeles, California
Client: California State Parks
Dates: 2006
Size: 32 acres
Architect: Michael Maltzan Architecture
Interpretive Planner: Ralph Appelbaum
Associates
Associate Landscape Architect:
Katherine Spitz Associates
Associate Urban Design: Arthur Golding

Project: Governor's Island
Location: New York, New York
Client: Governors Island Preservation
& Education Corporation (GIPEC)
Dates: 2006-2007
Size: 172 acres
Architect: Michael Maltzan Architecture
Structural Engineer: Guy Nordenson
and Associates

Project: Magok Waterfront
Location: Seoul, South Korea
Client: City of Seoul

Dates: 2008
Size: 200 acres
Architect: Office dA
Associate Landscape Architect: Group Han

Project: Shelby Farms Park
Location: Memphis, Tennessee
Client: Shelby Farms Park Conservancy
Dates: 2007-2008
Size: 4500 acres
Architect: Michael Maltzan Architecture

Project: Hudson Park and Boulevard Competition
Location: New York, New York
Client: Hudson Yards Development Corporation
Dates: 2008
Size: 4 acres
Architect: TEN Arquitectos, James Carpenter
Design Associates
Artist: James Carpenter

FIRM PROFILE

Hargreaves Associates is a professional consulting firm comprised of landscape architects and planners with offices in San Francisco, California; Cambridge, Massachusetts; New York City; and London, UK. The firm has been on the forefront of landscape architectural practice since its founding in 1983.

PRINCIPALS

Senior Principals:
George Hargreaves
Mary Margaret Jones

Principals:
Glenn Allen
Gavin McMillan
Kirt Rieder
Catherine Miller
Ken Haines
Jacob Petersen
Brian Jencek
Alan Lewis

George Hargreaves is Design Director and Senior Principal of Hargreaves Associates. Hargreaves received his BLA Magna Cum Laude from the University of Georgia, School of Environmental Design in 1977, and his MLA with Distinction from the Harvard University Graduate School of Design in 1979. He taught there for 20 years, tenured for 12 years as the Peter Louis Hornbeck Professor in Practice of Landscape Architecture, and served as the Department Chairman from 1996 to 2003. Hargreaves is a Fellow in the American Society of Landscape Architects. His work, and the work of Hargreaves Associates, has been published and exhibited internationally. In 2009, Hargreaves was the Mercedes T. and Sid R. Bass Landscape Architect in Residence at the American Academy of Rome. He has sat on numerous major juries and boards, including the Burnham Memorial Design Competition, Chair of the International Design Competition for Seoul Yeouido Riverside Park, Chair of the US President's Award for Urban Design and Landscape Architecture, the Editorial Advisory Board for Landscape Architecture Magazine and the American Academy in Rome Prize. He is the co-editor and author of *Large Parks* (Princeton Architectural Press, 2007).

Anita Berrizbeitia is professor of landscape architecture at the Harvard University Graduate School of Design. Her research focuses on contemporary and twentieth-century design and theory. She studied architecture at the Universidad Simón Bolívar, received a BA from Wellesley College and an MLA from the Harvard University Graduate School of Design. Berrizbeitia is the editor of Michael Van Valkenburgh Associates: Reconstructing Urban Landscapes (Yale University Press 2009), winner of a 2009 ASLA Honor Award in Communications. She is the author of Roberto Burle Marx in Caracas: Parque del Este 1956-1961 (University of Pennsylvania Press, 2004), for which she received the J.B. Jackson Book Prize in 2007 and, with architect Linda Pollak, of INSIDE/OUTSIDE: Between Architecture and Landscape (Rockport 1999).

Julia Czerniak is a registered landscape architect and founder and principal, with Mark Linder, of CLEAR. She is an Associate Professor at Syracuse University School of Architecture. Educated both as an architect (Princeton University, MArch 1992) and landscape architect (Pennsylvania State University, BA 1984), her research and practice focus on the intersection of these disciplines. Czerniak is editor of two books, *Large Parks* (Princeton Architectural Press, 2007) and *Case: Downsview Park Toronto* (Prestel and Harvard Design School, 2001).

Liz Campbell Kelly is a landscape designer working in New York. She is co-author, with George Hargreaves, of *Interventions in Hydrology* in Topos 59. She is the co-founder and co-editor of topophilia.org, an online journal of landscape architecture. She received her MLA at the University of Pennsylvania School of Design in 2006, and received her BA in Art/Semiotics Brown University in 1999, which included a year of study at the AA School of Architecture in London 1997-98.

LANDSCAPE ALCHEMY
The Work of Hargreaves Associates
HARGREAVES ASSOCIATES

Copyright © 2009 ORO *editions*

ORO *editions*
Publishers of Architecture, Art, and Design
Gordon Goff – Publisher
USA: PO Box 998, Pt Reyes Station, CA 94956
Asia: Block 8, Lorong Bakar Batu #02-04, Singapore 348743

www.oroeditions.com
info@oroeditions.com

ISBN: 978-0-9795395-9-6

Graphic Design: Sally Roydhouse, Andrés Rodríguez Ruiz
Copy editing: Christyanna LaFaver
Production: Joanne Tan, Gordon Goff
Color Separation and Printing: ORO *editions* Pte Ltd

Text printed using offset sheetfed printing process in 5 color 157 gsm matte art paper; an off-line gloss spot varnish was applied
to all photographs. Case made using Toyo Saifu cotton cloth over 3.5mm boards.

ORO *editions* has made every effort to minimize the overall carbon footprint of this project. As part of this goal, ORO *editions*,
in association with Global ReLeaf, have arranged to plant two trees for each and every tree used in the manufacturing of the paper
produced for this book. Global ReLeaf is an international campaign run by American Forests, the nation's oldest nonprofit conservation
organization. Global ReLeaf is American Forests' education and action program that helps individuals, organizations, agencies, and
corporations improve the local and global environment by planting and caring for trees.

DATE DUE
